Fifty Days

for an

Enduring Vision

A FIFTY-DAY DEVOTIONAL FOR A FOUNDATION BUILT ON SOLID BIBLICAL PRINCIPLES

Rick Joyner

MorningStar Publications
Division of MorningStar Fellowship Church
P.O. Box 19409, Charlotte, NC 28219-9409

Fifty Days for an Enduring Vision
Copyright © 2002 by Rick Joyner

Published by MorningStar Publications, a division of MorningStar Fellowship Church
P.O. Box 19409, Charlotte, NC 28219-9409

International Standard Book Number 1-929371-17-9.

MorningStar's website: www.morningstarministries.org
For information call 704-522-8111.

Unless otherwise stated, all Scripture quotations are taken from the New American Standard Bible, copyright © 1960, 1962, 1963, 1968, 1971, 1973, 1974, 1977 by The Lockman Foundation. Italics in Scripture reference for emphasis only.

Cover Design by Micah Davis
Book Layout by Dana Zondory

Table of Contents

Introduction

There is nothing on this earth as exciting, as exalted, or as fulfilling as the true Christian life. It is the most noble cause, the most lofty purpose, and the essence of the high calling that man was created for. In this book we will pursue a higher perspective of this most glorious quest—the Christian life.

This is the third book in a series that will ultimately be seven books. The goal of this series is to impart both faith and vision for believers to discern, understand, and walk in the purpose for which they are upon this earth. To accomplish this, we are seeking to establish our faith, vision, and therefore our lives on rock solid, biblical truth.

Recently, I was given a sobering vision of multitudes of mountain climbers. They were climbing toward the glory of God. However, most were falling off the mountain. They would all fall to the level where they had a stake firmly driven into the rock. As I watched I saw why they were falling. When they were driving their stakes into the rock face to fasten their safety ropes, they were driving them in only an inch or two. When one of these stakes gave way, large numbers of people who were all connected, fell together. Most seemed to be falling all the way to their death because they did not have any stakes driven in securely. I knew immediately the message of this vision was that we had to drive the stakes of truth much deeper into the rock. The higher we are to go, the more people these stakes are to hold, and the deeper they will have to be driven into the rock.

Contrary to some news reports, Islam is not the fastest growing religion—Christianity is by a large margin. However, while multitudes are coming to faith in Christ each day, many are also falling away. Many others are barely hanging on to the faith with their spiritual condition growing ever more precarious. Why? As the Lord warned in the Parable of the Sower, they lack depth, and the seed that is planted in them is easily stolen, destroyed by the heat of persecution, or choked out by the cares of this world.

While each of these successive books is seeking to impart an increasingly lofty vision of our purpose in Christ, we are also seeking to sink our roots ever more deeply into the biblical truths that are the foundation of our faith. This is essential if we are going to safely climb to the heights to which we are called. This was also the wise pattern that we see used by all of the New Testament writers—to impart vision while strengthening the foundations.

To drive these stakes of truth ever more deeply into the rock requires much more than just repeating truth. We need a deeper revelation and understanding of even the most basic Christian doctrines. There is yet more revelation and understanding to be gained about the cross and the atonement of Christ than possibly any Christian has ever fathomed. There is no greater revelation of God's love for man, or His severity, than the cross. Thankfully, we do not have to understand everything about the cross to trust it for our salvation. However, the more deeply we understand it, the more secure our faith will be when tried by the tests that will surely come. This is also necessary to carry the weight of walking in the power and glory of our high calling in Christ—to be His ambassadors and agents on this earth.

It is for this purpose that I began writing these books in the Fifty Days series. A foundation was laid in the first one that each additional book builds upon. They are also written so even a new believer can start with any volume and understand it. However, for the maximum benefit they should be read in sequence. Each succeeding book also drives deeper some of the foundational truths previously established. The deeper and more secure these truths are driven home, the more authority we can be trusted with, and the more people we may be able to help climb the mountain.

For this reason, when you see the redundancies and inherent reviews in this book, do not just pass over them. If you do, you will miss additional insights that are added to them which can strengthen these truths in your life. Ask the Lord for the grace to comprehend them deeper—not just believe in them, but to also live them. In the end we are not going to be judged on what we believed, but by what we lived.

It is for this reason that we are told in Romans 10:10, **"for with the heart man believes, resulting in righteousness...."** True faith is not just an intellectual assent with certain biblical and historic facts. The demons believe those. The faith that results in righteousness is from the heart, or the innermost being. What we live is what we really believe. Therefore, with all of these biblical truths, we are seeking to have them become more than something we believe in our minds, but truths that are driven ever deeper into our hearts so that they are our life.

DAY 1

Walking Into the Glory

There are progressive steps to maturity in Jesus Christ. These steps are outlined several times in Scripture, yet it seems that few Christians even know about them, much less follow the course where they lead. The failure to know these steps is probably the greatest reason for the defeat of those who fail to walk in a victorious Christian life. Our goal is to first see and understand these steps to maturity, while beginning the ascent up the mountain of the Lord, conquering ourselves and the enemies assigned to thwart us. At the same time, we must grow in vision, faith, and power which is the sure result of maturity in Christ.

The first step toward the success of any journey is to understand where we are going. What is our destination in Christ? Simply put, it is to have our intimate relationship with God restored, to become like Him, and to do the works that He did. Also necessary to successfully navigate to our destination is knowing where we started from. A map with the destination clearly marked will not do us any good unless we know where we are presently located on the map. So these two matters are foremost as we begin—first understanding where we are going, and then understanding where our starting point is.

The fall of man was the result of our first parents disobeying the commandment of the Lord. Disobedience was then sown into the fabric of man's nature. If you read the first two chapters in the Bible, and then the last two, you have the complete story. Everything between those two chapters deals with one essential subject—redemption. The goal of redemption is to restore man to his original condition before the fall, which is walking with God, obeying Him, and fulfilling His mandate to rule over the earth.

However, by the unfathomable riches of God's grace, He also established that He would not only restore man to the condition from which he had fallen, but raise him up as a glorious "new creation." This new creation man was to be much more than simply restored to the condition of the first Adam.

God walked with Adam in the garden, but the new creation man actually has God living in him! God has actually made man His temple and God now dwells in man! This is so glorious that it is often difficult even for those who have tasted the gift of salvation to fully comprehend.

The Lord created man for His pleasure, and the Lord's pleasure comes from having fellowship with men. He loved walking with Adam, teaching, and listening to him. This was the most tragic loss of the fall—man's relationship to God. The ultimate purpose of redemption is the restoration of that relationship. That is why the Bible is composed almost entirely of stories of how the Lord has related to men and women in this redemption process. The ultimate quest of every Christian life is therefore to be the intimate friend of the Lord. If there is any way we can measure true Christian maturity, it will be by how close we are to God.

Moses had one of the most special relationships with God that any man has had. An example of this relationship is found in Exodus 33:9-11:

> **And it came about, whenever Moses entered the tent, the pillar of cloud would descend and stand at the entrance of the tent; and the LORD would speak with Moses.**
> **When all the people saw the pillar of cloud standing at the entrance of the tent, all the people would arise and worship, each at the entrance of his tent.**
> **Thus the LORD used to speak to Moses face to face, just as a man speaks to his friend.**

Think how wonderful it would be if every time we wanted to speak with the Lord, He would descend from heaven and speak with us face to face just like He did with Moses. Do you think that would make your prayer life a little more exciting? However, the Scripture states that what we have in the New Covenant is even better than the relationship Moses had with the Lord, as we see in II Corinthians 3:7-10:

> **But if the ministry of death, in letters engraved on stones, came with glory, so that the sons of Israel could not look intently at the face of Moses because of the glory of his face, fading as it was,**
> **how shall the ministry of the Spirit fail to be even more with glory?**
> **For if the ministry of condemnation has glory, much more does the ministry of righteousness abound in glory.**

For indeed what had glory, in this case has no glory on account of the glory that surpasses it.

Here we see that the glory of what we have been given in the New Covenant is so great that what Moses had, even the visible glory that reflected from his face, can hardly be compared to it! We do not just meet with God face to face—we have Him living inside of us! He does not just descend to meet with us—He dwells with us continually.

Because Moses met with God face to face, His face shone with the glory of God. However, since God dwells inside of us, our whole lives should reflect His glory, not just our skin, but in everything we do. This is our calling—to be His temple, the place where His glory is manifested. This is our quest, which is more than understanding it—it is doing it. Our maturity will be reflected by how much of His glory is manifested through our lives. The reality of this should be just as clear on Monday morning as it is on Sunday morning.

We are going to study the progressive steps to maturity in this calling. I will lay an outline, and occasionally give references to other works for a more extensive study. However, we must always keep in mind that our goal is not just to study, but to walk in the maturity of our calling.

Notes:

DAY 2

Climbing the Mountain of God

On Day One we discussed the progressive steps to maturity in Jesus Christ. If followed, these steps will lead to a mature, victorious Christian life. Our goal as stated in Ephesians 4:15, is to **"...grow up in all aspects into Him, who is the head, even Christ."** To help those of you who want to run ahead a little bit, I will lay out a few of the places where these steps are found in Scripture so that you may begin the individual study of them. The first of these is addressed by the apostle Paul in I Corinthians 10:1-11:

> **For I do not want you to be unaware, brethren, that our fathers were all under the cloud, and all passed through the sea;**
>
> **and all were baptized into Moses in the cloud and in the sea;**
>
> **and all ate the same spiritual food;**
>
> **and all drank the same spiritual drink, for they were drinking from a spiritual rock which followed them; and the rock was Christ.**
>
> **Nevertheless, with most of them God was not well-pleased; for they were laid low in the wilderness.**
>
> **Now these things happened as examples for us, that we should not crave evil things, as they also craved.**
>
> **And do not be idolaters, as some of them were; as it is written, "The people sat down to eat and drink, and stood up to play."**
>
> **Nor let us act immorally, as some of them did, and twenty-three thousand fell in one day.**
>
> **Nor let us try the Lord, as some of them did, and were destroyed by the serpents.**
>
> **Nor grumble, as some of them did, and were destroyed by the destroyer.**
>
> **Now these things happened to them as an example, and they were written for our instruction, upon whom the ends of the ages have come.**

In this whole story we see the step-by-step procedure for God's people first being delivered from bondage. This takes place with the institution of the Passover, which was a prophetic model of the sacrifice of Jesus that delivers us from the power of the evil one. After being "baptized in the Red Sea" (verse 2), they are then taken on a step-by-step journey through the wilderness that is intended to mature and prepare them to possess their inheritance. (For those who are interested in an in-depth study of this outline to maturity, this is the subject matter of my book, *The Journey Begins*.)

Another outline is seen in the tabernacle itself. After entering the door, which represents Jesus (see John 10:7), the furniture of the tabernacle is laid out as a step-by-step progression into the very presence and glory of the Lord. This is the most comprehensive study of all, and we will look at it in depth in this book. You can also see a progression in the successive tabernacles and temples built for the Lord, culminating in the Lord Jesus Himself, and then in His church.

There are other places where you can see progressions toward maturity, such as the establishing of David's kingdom and the bringing of the Ark of God to Jerusalem. We see another in the Songs of Ascents (see Psalms 120 through 134), and then we have the very basic and practical outline for maturity given to us in II Peter 1:2-10:

> **Grace and peace be multiplied to you in the knowledge of God and of Jesus our Lord;**
> **seeing that His divine power has granted to us everything pertaining to life and godliness, through the true knowledge of Him who called us by His own glory and excellence.**
> **For by these He has granted to us His precious and magnificent promises, in order that by them you might become partakers of the divine nature, having escaped the corruption that is in the world by lust.**
> **Now for this very reason also, applying all diligence, in your faith supply moral excellence, and in your moral excellence, knowledge;**
> **and in your knowledge, self-control, and in your self-control, perseverance, and in your perseverance, godliness;**
> **and in your godliness, brotherly kindness, and in your brotherly kindness, love.**
> **For if these qualities are yours and are increasing, they render you neither useless nor unfruitful in the true knowledge of our Lord Jesus Christ.**

For he who lacks these qualities is blind or short-sighted, having forgotten his purification from his former sins.

Therefore, brethren, be all the more diligent to make certain about His calling and choosing you; for as long as you practice these things, you will never stumble.

Think of that. If these qualities are ours, and are increasing, we can be certain of our calling, and we will never stumble.

These are some of the more obvious ways that we see progressions toward maturity in our faith. If we are going to go on to maturity, we must have a vision of where we are going, know where we are, and be able to clearly see the next step. That is my primary goal for this book. My prayer is that all of us can see measurable, dramatic, progress in our faith and knowledge of the Lord, as well as the revelation of His glory, power, and His ways to enable us to impact a world progressing in darkness.

Notes:

DAY 3

The Journey Begins

On Day Two we saw how Paul described the wilderness journey of Israel in I Corinthians 10:1-11 as a parallel of our journey as Christians. He concluded his insights here with: **"Now these things happened to them as an example, and they were written for our instruction, upon whom the ends of the ages have come" (verse 11).** The experiences of Israel leaving Egypt, crossing the wilderness, and then possessing their promised land, is a step-by-step prophetic map of our journey toward the fulfillment of our calling in Christ. We start by being in bondage to this world, then we go through a place of training and learning the Lord's ways in a spiritual wilderness, before we are ready to actually start possessing our promises.

In our study, we want to examine this journey in increasing depth as a way to measure our own individual progress toward spiritual maturity. These principles can relate to us as individuals, as a congregation, or even to the universal church. We can see the church following this same pattern through history. This can help us to understand where we are, where we are going, and what the next step is. It can also give us confidence and speedy victories in our trials as we understand what the Lord is seeking to accomplish in us through them.

The first principle that we must understand is that as Christians we begin our journey from a place of spiritual bondage. Moses, who came to set God's people free, was a type or biblical model of Christ, who came to set us free. We can see a number of spiritual parallels in their lives. When Moses was born, the ruling power sought to destroy him by killing all the male babies. When Jesus was born, Herod did the same thing. As the Scriptures teach that there will be a revealing of the Lord through a glorious church at the end, we again see the ruling powers today trying to destroy the infants through abortion and other diabolical strategies.

The first time that Moses revealed himself to his brothers they rejected him, just as they would Christ the first time He came. When Moses returned, it was with great power to set God's people free, and to destroy all of the gods of Egypt. When Jesus returns He will not come again as a suffering Lamb, but as the conquering King. He will set His people free and destroy all the gods of this world while doing it.

In this scenario, Egypt is a type of the present world, and Pharaoh is a type of Satan, the ruler of this present world. Pharaoh did not let Israel go without a fight, and the Lord did not want him to. The Lord hardened his heart in order to make him a more accurate type of Satan, who will do everything he can to keep God's people in bondage.

When Moses first demanded that Pharaoh let Israel go, he not only refused, but commanded his taskmasters to increase the burdens on God's people, as we see in Exodus 5:9, **"Let the labor be heavier on the men, and let them work at it that they may pay no attention to false words."** We see here that Satan's first strategy in getting us to believe that God's promises are "false words" is to make our burdens heavier. When this happens, do not be discouraged, but encouraged. Just before we are about to be delivered by the power of God, the enemy always heaps the burdens on trying to get us to doubt God in this same way. The Word of God is sure, and we can also stand on His promise in I Corinthians 10:13:

> **No temptation has overtaken you but such as is common to man; and God is faithful, who will not allow you to be tempted beyond what you are able, but with the temptation will provide the way of escape also, that you may be able to endure it.**

Since we know that He will never allow us to be tempted beyond what we are able to bear, we can know our deliverance is near when it gets to that point.

We may ask, if the Lord has the power to destroy Satan, why doesn't He do it and make it easier for His people? The main reason is because He does not want to make it easy for His people. He wants to make it hard, and He wants every experience to be impressed upon us enough, so that for all of eternity we will remember the evils of sin, and His glorious ways as demonstrated through our deliverance.

As He said in Exodus 6:1, **"Then the LORD said to Moses, 'Now you shall see what I will do to Pharaoh; for under compulsion he shall let them go, and under compulsion he shall drive them out of his land.'"** The Lord wanted His people to know forever that they were not set free by the permission of Pharaoh (Satan), but by His power. The ruler of this world will never willingly let us go, but he will let us go. Power is coming.

16

When Moses began to demonstrate God's power through his staff, Pharaoh had his magicians duplicate this power, and they were able to up to a point. What is coming will be a very real power encounter. Satan can duplicate God's power up to a point, but then even the cults will begin to say like the magicians of Egypt "**...This is the finger of God**" **(Exodus 8:19).**

Even though God begins to demonstrate that His power is much greater than anything Satan can duplicate, this will not cause Satan to give up, just as Pharaoh remained stubborn. This will cause him to take an even more devious, and often more successful, strategy for keeping God's people under his yoke. We see him begin this in Exodus 8:25: "**And Pharaoh called for Moses and Aaron and said, "Go, sacrifice to your God within the land"** (of Egypt).

Once Satan knows that we are determined to serve the Lord, his next strategy will be to get us to compromise so that we try to worship the Lord while remaining in bondage to the ways of this world. Satan really doesn't mind us "having religion." What scares him is a single Christian really becoming free.

When Pharaoh saw that Moses was resolute he proposed another compromise, as we see in Exodus 8:28, "**And Pharaoh said, 'I will let you go, that you may sacrifice to the LORD your God in the wilderness; only you shall not go very far away. Make supplication for me.'**" Almost every new believer will hear from well-meaning friends and relatives, "It is good you have religion now—just don't go too far with it," meaning, "It is good to go to church on Sundays, but you have to live in the world, so don't become too radical." We too must be resolute that we are going to follow the Lord fully, going as far as He has called us to go.

After a few more power encounters, Pharaoh proposed one last compromise, as we see in Exodus 10:24, "**Then Pharaoh called to Moses, and said, 'Go, serve the LORD; only let your flocks and your herds be detained. Even your little ones may go with you.'**" Every believer will have to pass this same test.

If Satan sees that we are determined to go as far as God has called us to go, he will then try to get us to leave something behind under his domain. He knows very well that "**...where your treasure is, there will your heart be also**" **(Matthew 6:21),** so if we leave anything behind that is not carried all the way to God's Promised Land, we will at some point turn in our hearts back to the world, and end up back in bondage. Therefore, we must, like Moses, declare that "**...not a hoof will be left behind!**" **(Exodus 10:26).** From the very beginning of our walk with the Lord, we must learn it is crucial to have no compromise with the devil.

Notes:

DAY 4

Freedom

On Day Three we studied how Pharaoh is a type of Satan, the ruler of this present age, and how Egypt is a type of this present world. We also studied the resistance that Pharaoh gave to Moses when he demanded that the Lord's people be set free. This was pre-ordained by God because His people were not to be set free by the permission of Pharaoh, but by His power. Through all of the resistance, and the attempts by Pharaoh to get Moses to compromise the call of God, Moses remained resolute, declaring **"not a hoof"** that belonged to Israel would be left behind in Egypt. We must do the same if we are going to be free.

We can see in the book of Revelation how parallel plagues that are going to come upon the earth have the same ultimate purpose—to set the Lord's people free, as well as the rest of creation. Just as the plagues that came upon Egypt destroyed the gods of Egypt, the plagues that come upon the world will destroy the gods that men have made, and ultimately set men free.

There was one final plague that came upon Egypt which finally and completely set the Lord's people free from Egypt—the Passover. In I Corinthians 5:7 we read **"...for Christ our Passover also has been sacrificed."** The Passover was a biblical model of the sacrifice of Jesus that sets us free from bondage to this world. Let's look at a few of the ways that it gives us a powerful model of what the Lord Jesus did for us to set us free. These are taken from Exodus 12 (you may want to read this chapter before proceeding). We will start with verses 1-2:

> **Now the LORD said to Moses and Aaron in the land of Egypt,**
> **"This month shall be the beginning of months for you; it is**
> **to be the first month of the year to you."**

The Lord changed the entire Hebrew calendar so that the Passover would be the beginning of their year. This was to represent the new beginning that we have when we partake of the sacrifice of Jesus on the cross.

As we read in II Corinthians 5:17:

Therefore if any man is in Christ, he is a new creature; the old things passed away; behold, new things have come.

The night that Israel partook of the Passover, their whole world was to change. They were to leave the place that they had known their entire lives never to see it again. They were going to journey through places that they had never seen before. When they took the Passover, their whole world changed! When we partake of Christ, we are so radically changed that the only way to describe it is to say that we are "born again." We start all over. All things become new to us in a supernatural transformation.

However, there is one basic difference between what happened to Israel and what happens when we become a Christian. Israel's environment changed, but when we partake of Christ *we* change. Israel was taken out of Egypt, but in the New Covenant, Egypt is taken out of us—we become new. The world we are in may be the same, but the eyes we see it through are different.

This is one of the most precious Christian truths—in Christ we have a new beginning. He wipes out all of our past failures. There is no other religion or philosophy in the world that has such grace and power to transform human beings. Even so, when we are born again, that is not the end of the matter, rather it is the beginning. We must grow up into spiritual maturity. Having our minds transformed is a process, but it would not be possible for such a transformation without the initial regeneration by the Holy Spirit that comes when we first embrace the cross. We are forgiven! We are new creatures in Christ!

That we are called "new creatures" in Christ actually means that we are a new species. This is something that we must grasp, but it seems that few Christians do. Those who are born again by the Spirit of God are no longer just human beings. Before the cross, men walked with God, but under the New Covenant God comes to live in us. That is why Jesus said in John 16:7:

But I tell you the truth, it is to your advantage that I go away; for if I do not go away, the Helper shall not come to you; but if I go, I will send Him to you.

Think of that. What could possibly be better than walking with Jesus the way that these disciples did? But He said it would be better for them if He went away so that the Helper, His Spirit could come! Even better than walking with God is to have God living inside of us! Now we do not go to His temple, we are His temple. Our quest in this life is to live in the reality of this greatest of Christian truths—God has made man His abode.

The goal of the new creation is not just to be restored to the sinless state that Adam enjoyed before the fall. That is the starting point. Our sin is removed at the cross of Jesus. This is not something we can do, but we can abide in Him in whom there is no sin. We are not trying to make ourselves perfect, we are trying to more perfectly abide in the One who abides in us. We do not look to ourselves for the power or the goodness, but we look to Him.

We may stumble and get back up, but we must keep our focus on the ultimate goal of our calling, which we see in Ephesians 4:15:

but speaking the truth in love, we are to grow up in all aspects into Him, who is the head, even Christ.

You were called to grow up in **"all aspects"** into Christ. You are called to be like Him and do the works that He did. This is our journey, our quest, and we must never settle for a lesser vision.

On Day Five we will continue to examine the power of the cross that sets us free from all bondage to this world and releases us into the most glorious quest in all of creation—Christlikeness.

Notes:

DAY 5

The Perfect One

Today we further our study of the Passover, which was judgment upon Egypt, but deliverance for God's people. In I Corinthians 5:7 we read **"...for Christ our Passover also has been sacrificed."** The Passover was a biblical model of the sacrifice of Jesus that sets us free from the bondage of this world. The first instruction the Lord gave concerning the Passover was that the Jews were to change their calendar so the month in which it took place was the first month of the year, to represent how the Passover would make a new beginning for them (see Exodus 12:1-2). This was a prophecy that when we partake of the Passover sacrifice of Jesus we become a **"new creation,"** and **"all things become new"** to us (see I Corinthians 5:17 NKJV). Now we will look at the next aspect of the Passover that illuminates what the cross accomplished for us in Exodus 12:3,5-6:

> **"Speak to all the congregation of Israel, saying, 'On the tenth of this month they are each one to take a lamb for themselves, according to their fathers' households, a lamb for each household.**
> **'Your lamb shall be an unblemished male a year old; you may take it from the sheep or from the goats.**
> **'And you shall keep it until the fourteenth day of the same month, then the whole assembly of the congregation of Israel is to kill it at twilight."**

Here we see that the lamb was to be taken into the house for five days before it was to be sacrificed. This was to be prophetic of how Jesus would enter Jerusalem five days before he was crucified. We also see that Jesus was crucified on the Day of Preparation for the Passover, and died that evening (see John 19:14). In Exodus 12:6 we also see that the lambs were to be killed at twilight. Because the Hebrew day begins in the evening, (6:00 p.m.), at the very time when all of Israel was slaying the typical Passover lambs, *the* Passover Lamb, Jesus, was dying on the cross right in their midst, perfectly fulfilling the type.

As we see in Exodus 12:5, the Passover lambs had to be an **"unblemished male."** This was to speak of the sinless nature of Jesus. The reason why the

Israelites were to take the lamb into their houses five days before the sacrifice was to thoroughly examine it for flaws. What did the Jewish leaders do to Jesus the entire five days that He was in Jerusalem before His crucifixion? They examined Him continually seeking to find fault so that they could condemn Him, but they found none. Even Pilate finally said, **"I find no fault in Him" (John 19:4 NKJV).** Jesus was the acceptable Passover sacrifice of God.

In Exodus 12:6 we read, **"... the whole assembly of the congregation of Israel is to kill it at twilight."** In Matthew 27:22 we read of the crowd gathered at the trial of Jesus, **"...They all said, 'Let Him be crucified!'"** In verse 25 it states, **"And all the people answered and said, 'His blood be on us and on our children!'"** This was not just a statement of how the Jewish people rejected Him, but about how He was being crucified for the sin of all men, and because all men have rejected Him.

As the Lord Himself declared in Matthew 25:40, **"...Truly I say to you, to the extent that you did it to one of these brothers of Mine, even the least of them, you did it to Me."** To the degree we have ever rejected even the least of the Lord's people, we have rejected Him. We may be appalled by how Judas betrayed the Lord, and Peter denied Him when He needed His friends the most, but to the degree we have ever betrayed one of the Lord's people, even the least of them, we have done it to Him. To the degree we have denied, or refused to associate with one of the Lord's people, even the least of them, even those who may have doctrinal error, or other problems, we have done it to Him.

Jesus was without blemish, perfect, but we are not. That is why He died for us. He even died for those who crucified Him. Regardless of the flaws or sins in our life, He will forgive us, and cleanse us. If we have denied Him or betrayed Him by denying or betraying any of His people, He will forgive us of that also. He forgave Peter, and He could have even forgiven Judas if he had returned to Him as Peter did. What made Judas incorrigible was that he hung himself. Obviously Judas felt great remorse at what he had done, but by hanging himself he tried to pay the price for his own sin.

When we try to pay the price for our own sins it can make us incorrigible or beyond help. By doing so, we refuse the grace of God at the cross. We must learn that, regardless of how great our mistakes are, we can never pay the price for our own sin. The cross alone is the propitiation for sin. To offer any other kind of penitence is an affront to the cross, and a statement that the cross is not enough, that we somehow must pay the price for this one. We must flee from all such delusions that there is anything we can do to pay the price for our own sin, and flee to the cross. There we will find grace and forgiveness from the Perfect One who is also perfect in love.

DAY 6

The Power of Sacrifice

On Day Five we drew a parallel of how Israel's first Passover was a foreshadowing of the sacrifice of Jesus on the cross. We began to examine the nature of our sin, and the perfect Lamb that was offered for our atonement. Here we want to take a little more time to examine and understand the power of sacrifice so that we can know the power of what He accomplished for us by His sacrifice.

Unfortunately, cults and satanic worshipers seem to understand this basic principle of the spiritual power of sacrifice better than most Christians. A remarkable biblical example of this is found in II Kings 3:26-27:

> **When the king of Moab saw that the battle was too fierce for him, he took with him 700 men who drew swords, to break through to the king of Edom; but they could not.**
> **Then he took his oldest son who was to reign in his place, and offered him as a burnt offering on the wall. And there came great wrath against Israel, and they departed from him and returned to their own land.**

Sacrifice has power. Evil sacrifices can release evil power just as this king understood. The greater the sacrifice the greater the power that is released. Had this king sacrificed a sheep or goat, or even a servant, it would not have had this kind of dramatic result. If this heathen king, who offered his son, released power, how much more did the sacrifice of God's own Son release power?

As the Scriptures declare, all of creation was made for the Son and through Him, and in Him all things hold together. There is nothing in this universe as precious as the Son of God. Nothing greater could be sacrificed. That is why the cross is the very power of God (see I Corinthians 1:18). There is no power greater in this universe than what is available to us through the cross of Jesus. If the Passover sacrifice of these lambs that were just a type or a prophecy of the coming cross of Jesus could set Israel free from the most powerful empire on earth at the time, how much more can the actual cross of Jesus set us free from our bondage?

All the combined power of all of the armies on earth could not compare with a single drop of the blood of Jesus. That power is available to us at the cross. That is why it only takes faith the size of a single mustard seed to move a mountain. The reason our "faith" falls so far short of accomplishing much is because it is almost always reduced to faith in our faith, instead of faith in the cross of Jesus.

Just as the purpose of the power of God as demonstrated through Moses was to first set Israel free, we often want to do great exploits with our faith before we have been delivered from our sin. As Christians we may remain in bondage to evil passions, evil desires, and the evil ways of this present evil age. However, if we do, we can never say that we have not been offered the power to be set free from them. For a Christian to say they do not have the power to overcome the sin and evil of their heart is to say that the evil is more powerful than the cross, which is an obvious insult to the cross. The power has been offered to us to be free. We can reject it, but we can never say that it has not been given to us. If we remain under the power of sin, it is our choice, because we choose sin over freedom. That is proof of who we really love and who we really serve.

There are a host of false doctrines that seek to turn believers away from the power of the cross, proclaiming that it is not possible to be free from the sin and evil passions of this world. Some seek to replace the cross of Jesus with human penitence. The devil knows well that these frivolous attempts to pay the price for our own sins are a profound affront to the cross of Jesus. Such foolishness actually empowers human sin by feeding human selfishness. The cross of Jesus is enough, and it alone can set us free.

As the great hymn so powerfully declares, it is "*nothing* but the blood of Jesus." We must never allow our trust to be put in anything else, because only the cross of Jesus can set us free and set us on the course to our Promised Land.

Of all of the studies that we have made, or will make, there are none more crucial than this one. If we will put our trust in the cross, the power of God will be released in our life. To this day the enemy of our souls still has a boast before all of creation—that God can forgive us of our sins, but He really does not have the power to deliver us from our sins. Before the end comes there will be a bride without spot or wrinkle that will prove to all of creation for all time that He not only has the power to forgive mankind, but He also has the power to change us. His sacrifice is so powerful that we will not only be restored to the condition of man before the fall, but the cross actually transforms us into a "new creation" that greatly transcends the original creation state of man. Therefore our goal is not to return to the state of the first Adam, but to abide in the "last Adam," who is Christ.

As the saying goes, "There is a ditch on either side of the path of life." The doctrines of human perfection can cause us to stumble just as much as those that declare there is not enough power in the cross to really change us. This is not about human perfection. The doctrines of human perfection are little more than feeble attempts to resurrect and heal our old nature. Our humanity must be reckoned as dead.

We will look at this in more depth, but for now let us settle in our hearts that there is no limit on the power of God that is available to us through the cross of Jesus. Let us also settle in our hearts that His sacrifice was enough, and anything we try to add to it by our attempts to pay for our own sins, by any means, is an insult to the cross (as established in Hebrews 9:26-10:14). If the sacrifice of the heathen king of Moab had such power, how much more power does the sacrifice of God's own Son have? The cross is the power of God, and if we want to have the power of God manifested in our daily lives, we must take up the cross daily. The power of God is available at the cross. Our trust must be in the cross of Jesus, alone, to set us free and release God's power in our life to live as He has called us to live.

<u>Notes:</u>

DAY 7

The Blood Must Be Applied

We have been studying the power of sacrifice, and especially the power of the sacrifice of the Son of God to deliver us from bondage, which was typified by the Passover. Now we will go on to another crucial aspect of the Passover, as we see in Exodus 12:7,13:

Moreover, they shall take some of the blood and put it on the two doorposts and on the lintel of the houses in which they eat it.

And the blood shall be a sign for you on the houses where you live; and when I see the blood I will pass over you, and no plague will befall you to destroy you when I strike the land of Egypt.

Just as the sentence of death was on every household that did not have the blood of the sacrificial, Passover lamb applied to their house, the same is true for all of humanity, as we read in Romans 5:12: **"Therefore, just as through one man sin entered into the world, and death through sin, and so death spread to all men, because all sinned."** Even so, God has given to the whole world a Passover Lamb whose blood will fully protect those who apply it to their life. As we read in Romans 5:8-10:

But God demonstrates His own love toward us, in that while we were yet sinners, Christ died for us.

Much more then, having now been justified by His blood, we shall be saved from the wrath of God through Him.

For if while we were enemies, we were reconciled to God through the death of His Son, much more, having been reconciled, we shall be saved by His life.

All Israel had to do to protect their families from the death that was going to sweep over Egypt that night was to apply the blood of the specified Passover lamb to their doorways. When the angel of death saw the blood, he

29

passed over them. Likewise, all we have to do to be delivered from the sentence of death that is upon all mankind is to apply the blood of the cross of Jesus to our lives. Nothing more will help, and nothing less will save us.

Israel would not have been saved by knowing that there had to be a Passover lamb sacrificed, or even to have sacrificed it, unless and until the blood was applied. Likewise, it does not do us any good just to know that there had to be a sacrifice for our sin. It does not even do us any good to know Jesus made that sacrifice, unless His blood is applied to our life. Just knowing the facts is not the same as trusting in them for salvation. Even the demons know the power of the cross. Salvation requires more than just an intellectual assent to the spiritual and historic facts of the cross, as Romans 10:8-10 states:

> **But what does it say? "The word is near you, in your mouth and in your heart"—that is, the word of faith which we are preaching,**
> **that if you confess with your mouth Jesus as Lord, and believe in your heart that God raised Him from the dead, you shall be saved;**
> **for with the heart man believes, resulting in righteousness, and with the mouth he confesses, resulting in salvation.**

There can be a big difference between believing with our minds and believing with our hearts. The belief that is required for salvation is more than just an intellectual assent to the facts. To believe with our heart is to believe with our life. Just as anyone passing through the Hebrew neighborhoods that night could see the blood had been applied to each house that had partaken of the Passover, if we have partaken of the Passover Lamb that is Christ, His blood will likewise be evident on our lives.

Jesus said, **"I am the way, and the truth and the life; no one comes to the Father, but through Me" (John 14:6).** The way is not a formula, but a Person. Knowing the truth is more than just having accurate doctrines—it is knowing a Person who must also be our life. If Jesus is not our life, we really do not know the way or the truth either. Salvation is much more than just agreeing that Jesus died on the cross for the sins of the world—it is embracing the cross and trusting in His atonement for the forgiveness of our own sin. Just as the Passover blood had to be applied to every house that was trusting in it for deliverance from death, the blood of Jesus must be applied personally to every life.

No one is going to be saved because they live in a "Christian" country. No one is going to be saved because they have a parent who knows the Lord. No one is even going to be saved because they go to church, or even because they were baptized, unless they have a personal faith in Him, and His blood is applied to their life. We must each have our own faith, and our own relationship to the Lord. If we do, the evidence of what has taken place in our heart will be clearly seen on the outside of our lives as well.

Just as we saw in our previous study, once Israel partook of the Passover, their whole world changed. They left Egypt immediately to go to a place they had never seen. Likewise, when we partake of the Passover sacrifice of Jesus everything changes—we are born again into a whole new world.

If you have been in church all of your life, and know very well all of the doctrines of salvation, but have never actually been born again by having a personal encounter with the Son of God, you can do so right now. All you have to do is humble yourself and confess your sins to God. Then ask Him to forgive you and cover you in the blood of His Son's sacrifice, knowing that there is nothing you can do to make atonement for yourself, but also knowing that His sacrifice is sufficient to cover your sins. This simple faith will allow you to be accepted by the Father into His own household. Then ask Him for the baptism in the Holy Spirit, who was given to lead us into all truth, so we might live lives that glorify the Son of God, by displaying the power of His sacrifice in our lives.

As we studied on Day Six, if the sacrifice of the king of Moab could release such power to cause the armies of Israel to flee, how much more power does the sacrifice of the Son of God have? His sacrifice is enough to cover all of your sins, to redeem you from the bondage of sin, and to give you eternal life. As we begin to comprehend this, we are transformed by the power of such great love.

> **For this reason, I bow my knees before the Father,**
> **from whom every family in heaven and on earth derives its name,**
> **that He would grant you, according to the riches of His glory, to be strengthened with power through His Spirit in the inner man;**
> **so that Christ may dwell in your hearts through faith; and that you, being rooted and grounded in love,**

may be able to comprehend with all the saints what is the breadth and length and height and depth,

and to know the love of Christ which surpasses knowledge, that you may be filled up to all the fulness of God.

Now to Him who is able to do exceeding abundantly beyond all that we ask or think, according to the power that works within us,

to Him be the glory in the church and in Christ Jesus to all generations forever and ever. Amen (Ephesians 3:14-21).

DAY 8

We Must Eat the Whole Thing

The main purpose of our study is to gain a clear understanding of our purpose in Christ and what we must do to accomplish it. For this reason we are examining the steps to maturity so we can understand where we are, and what we need to do next. Because the strength of the foundation will determine the strength and magnitude of what can be built upon it, we are taking the time to lay the foundation correctly. Without question, the strength of our spiritual life will be determined by the revelation, understanding, and application of the cross in our lives. As Paul wrote in I Corinthians 1:18:

For the word of the cross is to those who are perishing foolishness, but to us who are being saved it is the power of God.

We will know the power of God in our life to the degree that the cross has worked in our life. Therefore, let us continually seek to sink our roots deeper into the knowledge of what was accomplished for us at the cross, and to take up our cross and carry it daily. The life of the cross is foolishness to those who are perishing, but it is the salvation of God, the wisdom of God, the glory of God, and the power of God for those who are being saved.

Christ Jesus is called the Passover Lamb of God, and we have been studying the prophetic Passover sacrifice in Exodus to illustrate what the cross accomplished for us. In Exodus 12:8-11, we see several more important aspects of this feast and how Israel was commanded to eat it, which are crucial for us to understand.

And they shall eat the flesh that same night, roasted with fire, and they shall eat it with unleavened bread and bitter herbs.
Do not eat any of it raw or boiled at all with water, but rather roasted with fire, both its head and its legs along with its entrails.

> **And you shall not leave any of it over until morning, but whatever is left of it until morning, you shall burn with fire.**
>
> **Now you shall eat it in this manner: with your loins girded, your sandals on your feet, and your staff in your hand; and you shall eat it in haste—it is the LORD's Passover.**

The way they had to eat the Passover is summed up in these three points:

1) with bitter herbs and unleavened bread

2) they had to eat the whole thing

3) as they ate they had to be ready to depart in haste

Because points one and three are related, we will save them for the next study, but point two is worthy in itself of a life of pursuit—they had to eat the whole thing. One of the most dangerous compromises we could ever make in our life is to pick and choose which aspects of the gospel we are going to accept. This is possibly the one thing that has most weakened the church through the ages because it dilutes the very foundation of the power of the cross in our life.

If we come to Christ with any conditions as to what we will accept, or what we will do, we are not partaking of His atonement as He has prescribed. He will be the Lord of all, or not at all. Let us consider the following scriptures, beginning with what is called "The Great Commission" in Matthew 28:18-20:

> **And Jesus came up and spoke to them, saying, "All authority has been given to Me in heaven and on earth.**
>
> **Go therefore and make disciples of all the nations, baptizing them in the name of the Father and the Son and the Holy Spirit,**
>
> **teaching them to observe all that I commanded you; and lo, I am with you always, even to the end of the age."**

The basis for The Great Commission is **"all authority"** in heaven and earth has been given to Jesus. There is no place or person on earth that is beyond the exercise of His authority, if He chooses to exercise it. As King David wrote in Psalm 8:1, **"O LORD, our Lord, how majestic is Thy name in *all* the earth...."** In biblical times one's name was equated with their authority. There is no place on earth that belongs to the devil. As the scripture again asserts in Psalm 24:1: **"The earth is the LORD's, and *all* it contains, the world, and those who dwell in it."** This must also be our quest in seeking to carry out The Great Commission—to see His authority revealed in all of the earth. That is why the commission is to **"make disciples of *all* nations."**

The last part of that commission was to teach these nations to observe *all* that He has commanded us. This seems to have been the point made by the angel in Acts 5:19-20:

> **But an angel of the Lord during the night opened the gates of the prison, and taking them out he said,**
> **"Go your way, stand and speak to the people in the temple the whole message of this Life."**

If we are endeavoring to fulfill The Great Commission, to be ministers of the gospel, we must present the whole message of the gospel. It has been the tendency for those who have been entrusted with this Great Commission to omit, or overlook, what they do not understand or agree with. This has perpetually opened the door to weakness and even heresy in the church.

For this reason we must understand, embrace, and refuse to compromise II Timothy 3:16-17: *"All Scripture* **is inspired by God and profitable for teaching, for reproof, for correction, for training in righteousness; that the man of God may be adequate, equipped for every good work."**

If we are going to partake of the Lord's Passover, we must eat the whole thing. We cannot pick and choose what aspects of the gospel we are going to accept and what parts we are not. There are aspects to the cross and the gospel that are stumbling blocks to many, but if we start watering down the message, then we have stumbled over the whole. That which would cause us to pick and choose what we will obey and what we will not, was precisely the rationale for the first sin of mankind, and also what released death into the world in the first place. Redemption will only be complete when we determine to die completely to our own will in order to be fully obedient to Him. If we do not, we will continue to be open for further disobedience and its accompanying consequences—death.

Notes:

DAY 9

The Feast of Unleavened Bread

The next main aspect of the Passover Feast is the Feast of Unleavened Bread, which is a part of the Passover, as we read in Exodus 12:17:

> **You shall also observe the Feast of Unleavened Bread, for on this very day I brought your hosts out of the land of Egypt; therefore you shall observe this day throughout your generations as a permanent ordinance.**

In Scripture leaven speaks of two things. The first is malice and wickedness as we read in I Corinthians 5:8: **"Let us therefore celebrate the feast, not with old leaven, nor with the leaven of malice and wickedness, but with the unleavened bread of sincerity and truth."** The second thing that leaven speaks of is both the legalism of the Pharisees and the liberalism of the Sadducees, as the Lord warned in Matthew 16:6: **"And Jesus said to them, "Watch out and beware of the leaven of the Pharisees and Sadducees."**

The Feast of Unleavened Bread is celebrated in remembrance of *how* Israel came out of Egypt, and it is a revelation of how we keep unwanted leaven out of our lives. As we read in Deuteronomy 16:3:

> **You shall not eat leavened bread with it; seven days you shall eat with it unleavened bread, the bread of affliction (for you came out of the land of Egypt in haste), in order that you may remember all the days of your life the day when you came out of the land of Egypt.**

The reason Israel ate unleavened bread when they came out of Egypt was because as they fled Egypt "in haste," their bread did not have time to become leavened. This is also how we keep the leaven of malice and wickedness, legalism, or liberalism out of our lives—when we partake of the Passover sacrifice of Christ we must flee the world and worldliness with such haste that leaven does not have time to spring up in us.

One of the basic characteristics of a true Christian life is that it is moving, flowing, and going somewhere. The River of Life was not called a lake, but a "river" because a river is flowing and moving toward a certain destination. As a river gets closer to its destination it usually becomes wider and deeper. Just as water is sometimes used as a metaphor for truth in Scripture, all truth must be moving and growing becoming both more expansive and deeper for us.

In the very first mention of the Holy Spirit in Scripture (see Genesis 1:2) we see that He is *moving*. Nowhere does it say that He stopped. Moving is His nature, which is why His acts are often called a "move of the Holy Spirit." As Paul said in Acts 17:28, **"for in Him we live and *move*...."** This is how we keep the leaven out of our lives. When any of that which is called leaven begins to creep into a Christian's life, it will almost always be the result of them having stopped growing and moving toward their destiny in Christ.

The children of Israel were required to celebrate this Feast of Unleavened Bread each year with the Passover to remind them of how they left the land of Egypt in such haste that their bread did not have time to become leavened. We too need this constant reminder. Just as water that stops moving will quickly become contaminated, our faith must be ever moving and growing if it is to stay pure.

Just as the greatest opposition to the Lord Jesus when He walked the earth was from the Pharisees and Sadducees, there is a constant attack upon every Christian to turn aside from the River of Life and begin to follow the traditions of men, worshiping what God did in the past rather than what He is doing now. We must honor the great things the Lord has done, and our fathers and mothers in the Lord whom He used to do them through, but we must write our own history.

Christianity is the greatest quest, with the greatest destiny. How could we ever find anything more worthy than the pursuit of God, growing in the knowledge of His ways, and the devotion to do His will?

DAY 10

The Sheaf of the First Fruits

As we have studied in Exodus 12, the Passover Lamb was to be taken into the house five days before it was to be sacrificed. During that time the people were to examine it for any flaws because the Passover of the Lord had to be a lamb without blemish. As we are told in Matthew 11:13, **"...the Law prophesied until John."** This was a prophecy of how Christ, "our Passover," was to enter Jerusalem five days before He was to be crucified.

As Jesus was entering Jerusalem, Jews all over the city were taking the Passover lambs into their houses in preparation for the feast. During the five days when all of the people were examining their Passover lambs, the priests, Pharisees, and Sadducees examined Jesus continually seeking to find any flaw in Him, and they could not. Since the Jewish day begins with evening and Jesus was crucified on the Day of Preparation for the Passover, at the very time Jesus was dying on the cross, Jews all over the city were putting the knives to their Passover lambs.

In Leviticus 23 we have another ritual which was to be performed after the Sabbath of the Passover (all days in which there was to be no laborious work were also called Sabbaths). This was called "the waving of the sheaf of the first fruits." This ritual required the **"the sons of Israel"** to go out and gather a sheaf of the first fruits, which at that time of the year were just beginning to sprout. Then they delivered it to the priest who brought it before the Lord and waved it. After the Passover on which the Lord was crucified, at the very time when the priest was waving this "sheaf of the first fruits," Jesus was coming forth from the grave, the first fruits of the resurrection. This "sheaf of the first fruits," was the promise of a great harvest to come.

Only a few people in Israel understood the significance of what was happening in their midst on that fateful Passover. Even the Lord's disciples did not seem to fully comprehend it. However, as we look back at how perfectly the Lord fulfills His Word, always perfectly on time, we can have confidence in the unfathomable promises He has given to us. The Lord is always faithful, and He is always on time.

The fact that the Lord would send His own Son to die for our sins is a marvel that all of creation will certainly be in awe of for all eternity. That He would also give us the promise of eternal life, and just as He raised His own Son, He will raise us from the dead so we may ever live before Him, is another wonder of wonders. This is the hope that empowers us to live beyond the cares of this present world and for the gospel of the age to come. As we read in Hebrews 12:1-2:

> **Therefore, since we have so great a cloud of witnesses surrounding us, let us also lay aside every encumbrance, and the sin which so easily entangles us, and let us run with endurance the race that is set before us,**
>
> **fixing our eyes on Jesus, the author and perfecter of faith, who for the joy set before Him endured the cross, despising the shame, and has sat down at the right hand of the throne of God.**

Just as it was the hope of the resurrection and the glory that He was to receive that enabled Jesus to endure the cross, it is the truth of the resurrection that empowers all of the sacrifices that we, too, may be called to make for the sake of this gospel. The knowledge of the resurrection has sustained and empowered the martyrs of every age, and it is as we behold the glory which is set before us that we are able to take up our cross and "die daily."

The ultimate fear by which the enemy has mankind in bondage is the fear of death. It is the truth of the resurrection that breaks this ultimate bondage, and truly sets us free from the powers of this present evil age to live by the power of the age to come. As we are set free in this way, we no longer live for the things that are temporary, but for the eternal. In this way we die to this world. If we are dead to the world, there is nothing this world can do to us. This is the greatest freedom we can ever know on earth, and it is this freedom that the enemy fears more than any other. Those who are already dead have nothing to fear—those who are already dead will therefore be fearless in standing for the truth of the gospel. Their very fearlessness is an irresistible witness of the resurrection.

We are called to live a life that is free from fear, and we are called to live by faith. The linchpin of faith is our faith in the resurrection. The cross displayed for all time the great love that God has for us. The resurrection magnifies it. If God loves us this much, then whom should we fear?

We will continue to examine the resurrection, this great foundation of our faith, that we might live in the victory that was gained for us, having been liberated from every fear.

DAY 11

The Resurrection

We have studied how it was the hope of the resurrection and the glory He was to receive which enabled Jesus to endure the cross. It has also been the truth of the resurrection that empowered all of the martyrs of every age, and it is as we behold the glory set before us that we are able to take up our crosses and "die daily."

We must also consider, if the ultimate fear by which the enemy has kept mankind in bondage is the fear of death, and the truth of the resurrection breaks this bondage, why is the world in such darkness and bondage? It is because the church has been almost mute on this greatest of truths since the first century.

The great preacher, Spurgeon, once made a remarkable statement that very few Christians believe in the resurrection. When I read this, I thought it must have been a misprint, but I felt the Spirit witness to me that it was true. It is not believing in our *minds* which results in righteousness, but believing in our *hearts* (see Romans 10:10). It is not by just believing in the doctrine of the resurrection that we are set free, but when we believe in our hearts so it changes the way that we live and view this present world. If we truly believed in the resurrection in our hearts, most of our lives would be very different than they are now. We would not be so consumed with the things that are passing away and would give ourselves wholly to that which is eternal.

The greatest freedom we can ever know on this earth is not to be bound by fear. The way we are freed from fear is by dying to this world through the cross of Jesus. What can you do to a dead man? A dead man does not fear, does not take into account wrongs suffered, etc. If we are dead to this world, there is nothing that the world can do to us, and we will therefore be the freest people on earth. This does not mean that we do not manage properly whatever this life has entrusted to us, but we do it in faith as unto the Lord, not in fear. Such fearlessness is an irresistible witness of the resurrection. Why don't we proclaim and display this more? Because faith is not yet in our hearts.

In Acts 1:2, we see that the office of the apostle was given to be a witness of His *resurrection*. In Acts 4:33, we read that power was given to witness of His *resurrection*. In Romans 1:4, we are told that Jesus **"...was declared the Son of God with power by the resurrection from the dead...."** The message of the resurrection is central to true faith, and is, with the cross, the central message of Christianity. The message of the cross is of no real effect without the message of the resurrection, as Paul wrote in I Corinthians 15:13-14:

> **But if there is no resurrection of the dead, not even Christ has been raised;**
> **and if Christ has not been raised, then our preaching is vain, your faith also is vain.**

After reading Spurgeon's statement about how there were not many Christians who believed in the resurrection, I searched my library for the messages on the resurrection written by the great saints of history. I was astonished at what I found—those whose writings included many volumes, would sometimes have only a couple of pages devoted to this most powerful truth. None seemed to give it more than lip service, or the obligatory Easter sermon. Could this be why so much of the church has lost its power? I think so. In Acts 4:1-2 we see why this great truth has fallen into such neglect:

> **And as they were speaking to the people, the priests and the captain of the temple guard, and the Sadducees, came upon them,**
> **being greatly disturbed because they were teaching the people and proclaiming in Jesus the resurrection from the dead.**

In Acts 23:6, Paul declared before the same council that he was **"...on trial for the hope and resurrection of the dead!"** It was preaching the *resurrection* that incited the persecution against the church. This is the one message that the enemy cannot stand because it threatens the very root of his power over men—the fear of death. However, we will never be an apostolic church until this central theme of the apostolic gospel is recovered, and we resolve to stand boldly for the truth of the resurrection. If we believe, we will certainly rise again. If we believe, our lives will demonstrate our faith.

DAY 12

The Power of Resurrection Life

The cross and resurrection are foundational doctrines of Christianity. They are intertwined and cannot be separated from one another. We cannot experience resurrection without first dying. The degree to which we lay down our lives for the Lord and His purposes, while embracing His cross, is the same degree that we will experience His resurrection life, perceiving and partaking of the glory that He now abides in.

Jesus did not stop at the cross, and it is imperative that we not stop at the cross. The Lord did not just call Israel out of Egypt, but He called them into the Promised Land. We are not just called to die to this world, but we are called to walk in a glorious new creation.

However, just as Israel had to go through a wilderness that was the exact opposite of the land of milk and honey they had been promised in order to get to their inheritance, we too, must do the same. As the Lord said in John 16:33:

> **"These things I have spoken to you, that in Me you may have peace. In the world you have tribulation, but take courage; I have overcome the world."**

As the apostle Paul affirmed in Acts 14:22, **"...Through many tribulations we must enter the kingdom of God."** We go through trials, which are all meant to strengthen our faith and character, so we can be trusted with the authority and treasures of the age to come. This is why Paul wrote in Romans 5:3-5:

> **And not only this, but we also exult in our tribulations, knowing that tribulation brings about perseverance;**
>
> **and perseverance, proven character; and proven character, hope;**
>
> **and hope does not disappoint, because the love of God has been poured out within our hearts through the Holy Spirit who was given to us.**

Here we see a progression towards proven character and the hope that does not disappoint, but begins with tribulation. In this world we will have trials and tribulations, but they are allowed so we can experience the power and authority of resurrection life. Every cross we have to bear will lead to a greater glory. We must go through a wilderness to get to our Promised Land. The wilderness is designed to work in us that which will enable us to possess the promises of God, and to be trusted with the power and authority He has called us to walk in, which demonstrates His authority, power, and dominion.

The purpose of our Promised Land is not just to allow us to have the good life, but rather to demonstrate the nature of the Lord's kingdom and ways to a fallen world. The greatest demonstration of the Lord's kingdom was the Lord's own life. He had dominion over the earth, and over the works of the devil. He says in John 17:18, **"As Thou didst send Me into the world, I also have sent them into the world."**

Jesus demonstrated the power of a life in harmony with the Father. We are called to demonstrate the power of a life that is likewise in unity with Him by abiding in the Son. Jesus walked in power over all diseases, and we are called to do the same. In Luke 10:19, we see that the Lord gave His disciples authority over **"all the power of the enemy."** However, is there anyone who is walking in this? I do not know of anyone who can presently bind all of the evil in a single place, much less all of his power. However, I know many that are growing in authority over evil spirits, and are through prayer and proclamation of the truth changing the spiritual atmosphere over their regions. This is the authority that we are called to grow in.

Our goal is to be like Jesus and to do the works that He did. We cannot do this on our own, but only by abiding in Him. We learn to abide in Him by going to the cross. It seems that almost everyone wanted to be close to Jesus to experience the miracles and glory of His works, but when He went to the cross even His closest disciples fled from Him, because they did not yet understand the resurrection. After the resurrection, however, even these proved willing to face death with the greatest courage and peace.

The degree to which we will abide in Him will be determined by the degree to which we behold the power of His resurrection—the power, glory, and authority that He has now. When we know He is in control, and that nothing can happen to us that He does not allow for our own good, then we will not flee from the cross—we will count it all joy when we, too, are able to suffer for His name's sake. There is no greater privilege that we can be given in this life, and such is the path to unfathomable glory. Do not waste your trials, but as the great apostle declared in Philippians 3:7-14:

> **But whatever things were gain to me, those things I have counted as loss for the sake of Christ.**
>
> **More than that, I count all things to be loss in view of the surpassing value of knowing Christ Jesus my Lord, for whom I have suffered the loss of all things, and count them but rubbish in order that I may gain Christ,**
>
> **and may be found in Him, not having a righteousness of my own derived from the Law, but that which is through faith in Christ, the righteousness which comes from God on the basis of faith,**
>
> **that I may know Him, and the power of His resurrection and the fellowship of His sufferings, being conformed to His death;**
>
> **in order that I may attain to the resurrection from the dead.**
>
> **Not that I have already obtained it, or have already become perfect, but I press on in order that I may lay hold of that for which also I was laid hold of by Christ Jesus.**
>
> **Brethren, I do not regard myself as having laid hold of it yet; but one thing I do: forgetting what lies behind and reaching forward to what lies ahead,**
>
> **I press on toward the goal for the prize of the upward call of God in Christ Jesus.**

After leaving Egypt, all the experiences that Israel went through were to prepare them for the high calling of representing the Lord on earth. We, too, have been given this highest of callings, and everything we go through is intended to prepare us for it. He wants us to do the works that He did and even greater ones, to demonstrate His resurrection and His authority which is above all authority. He is now looking for those who will endure the things that fashion our character, so He can trust us with this unprecedented honor. This is your destiny. You are a new creation.

Notes:

DAY 13

The Journey Continues

This Promised Land that we have in Christ is not just what we inherit after we die, but it is the glorious new creation that we become in this life. However, when you are born it is not the fulfillment of your life, but the beginning. Likewise, when you are born again, it is not the fulfillment of your calling, but the beginning of the glorious journey. There is no life so exciting, so wonderful, and so fulfilling as the Christian life. It is the greatest quest for the greatest souls to ever walk the earth.

The Lord did not call Israel just to get them out of Egypt, but in order to lead them into their inheritance. Israel had a very specific Promised Land, and so do we. What is the Christian Promised Land that we are called to inherit in this life? As we read before in I Corinthians 10:11, after Paul gave an outline of Israel's experience in the wilderness he said, **"Now these things happened to them as an example, and they were written for our instruction, upon whom the ends of the ages have come."** Israel's experience was a prophetic map, and a model, of both our journey and our inheritance in Christ. Let's look at a couple of basic parallels.

Israel's Promised Land was a relatively small nation, but it was in the middle of the emerging nations of the earth. It was to be a place where the Lord was worshiped and where the people lived by His ways. Their life was to be a striking contrast to the nations around them as a demonstration of how the Lord's ways were higher. Those who obeyed and served the Lord were to enjoy extraordinary benefits, such as: all of their diseases healed, long life, peace, joy, and prosperity. Because He also instituted commandments for cleansing the land, even nature would prosper because of the right-eousness and justice of those who would dwell in the land. This would result in an increased fruitfulness of the land.

Likewise, the Lord did not just save us so we can go to heaven, but so we can be a holy nation in the midst of the earth that testifies to the glory and power of the Lord and His ways. There are extraordinary and wonderful benefits for living under the domain of Christ. We are called to be witnesses of the power and glory of the kingdom of God by living in them now. It is a **"land flowing with milk and honey."** It is to be a blessing and wonder in the midst of this dark and confusing world. The seed of Abraham was called to be a blessing to all of the families on the face of the earth. This is our calling, to be a blessing to everyone around us.

In the New Covenant we find that the Lord gives His people authority over sickness and disease, as well as over all of the power of the evil one. We also see that Christians are called to a life of triumph and victory that gives glory to God and a revelation to the world of the Lord's victory on the cross. However, just as there was a journey that Israel had to make to get to their Promised Land, and then they had many battles to fight to possess it, the same is true with us. In a sense, the church has been making its journey through the wilderness since the first century. However, before the end of this age the church will possess its inheritance and live in it as a witness to all of the other "nations" on the face of the earth.

The wilderness that Israel crossed was essentially the exact opposite of the land they had been promised, so is our wilderness. They had been promised a land flowing with milk and honey, but in the wilderness they did not even have any water. However, it was this journey through the place that was so contrary to the promises, that they learned to trust in the provision of the Lord, and know the righteousness of His ways. The same is true with us.

The most important thing that happened in the wilderness was they received God's instructions, and they built Him a dwelling place so He could actually dwell in their very midst. The Lord's presence with them was the greatest inheritance of all. The greatest of all the blessings that we have gained through Christ is Christ Himself. We must also esteem His presence with us as the greatest treasure of all.

It has been said that Israel could have crossed the wilderness in only two weeks. That may be true, but it was a full two years before the Lord led them to the place where they could enter. He first had to give them His command-ments, teach them His ways, and complete His tabernacle so He could dwell in their midst. We, too, must learn to be patient when in the wilderness— between the place where we are called and where we begin to enter into our promises.

The wilderness is hard, but it is essential, and it can be a most glorious place of fellowship and getting to know the Lord. For us to be trusted with the full inheritance, we must know fully that He is the greatest inheritance that we could ever have. Therefore, our primary goal must always be greater than just possessing the promises—it must be to know the Lord, to worship Him, and to serve Him in all that we do.

It is much better to stay in the wilderness where we are compelled to experience Him and seek Him than to possess our promises. The inheritance we have in Christ is so wonderful that it can easily become an idol in itself, if our foundation is not right. That is why so few Christians have truly walked in the fullness of the promises we have in Christ. Some assert that none have walked in the fullness of the promises since the first century. That is debatable, but it seems obvious that none are today walking in all of the promises we have been given in Christ. This is probably because so many quickly begin to esteem the promises above the One who gives them.

This is why we are taking our time in this study and patiently reviewing many things. Our goal is not just to know about the Lord and our inheritance, but to know the Lord and possess our inheritance. To do this we must possess the wisdom to know that the Lord Himself is the greatest inheritance, and that our possession of any of His promises is so we can be a witness of His greatness and glory in the midst of the earth, not just so we can be blessed.

As we proceed by examining how Israel's wilderness journey parallels our own journey to maturity in Christ, we will find that many of the experiences we go through are meant to review and reiterate the truths that we learned by our deliverance from "Egypt." Each new experience is both a review and a step forward. In that way, the strongest foundation is laid and is continually re-fortified. Every single thing in our lives is intended to do the same for us.

One of our main goals in this study is to be able to quickly recognize every thing the Lord is using in our life in relation to what He wants to do in us. As we start to understand His work we will be more prone to work with Him, and thereby get out of the wilderness and into the Promised Land much faster. So let us go on to know the Lord, and possess our full inheritance in Him so the glory of His ways may be found in the midst of the earth as a witness to all.

Notes:

DAY 14

Go to Heaven, Now

Genesis 28:12-17 tells of a remarkable experience that Jacob had, which is also relevant to us today:

> And he had a dream, and behold, a ladder was set on the earth with its top reaching to heaven; and behold, the angels of God were ascending and descending on it.
>
> And behold, the LORD stood above it and said, "I am the LORD, the God of your father Abraham and the God of Isaac; the land on which you lie, I will give it to you and to your descendants.
>
> Your descendants shall also be like the dust of the earth, and you shall spread out to the west and to the east and to the north and to the south; and in you and in your descendants shall all the families of the earth be blessed.
>
> And behold, I am with you, and will keep you wherever you go, and will bring you back to this land; for I will not leave you until I have done what I have promised you."
>
> Then Jacob awoke from his sleep and said, "Surely the LORD is in this place, and I did not know it."
>
> And he was afraid and said, "How awesome is this place! This is none other than the house of God, and this is the gate of heaven."

The first point that we should observe here is that to Jacob the dream was real. Dreams can be a window into the heavenly realm. For this reason dreams have been one of the primary ways the Lord has spoken to His people from the beginning. In Acts 2, we see it will continue to be one of the primary ways that He speaks to us at the end. It is becoming increasingly crucial as we proceed toward the end of this age that we understand dreams, be able to discern those that are from the Lord from those that are not, and be able to interpret them.

The second point is that Jacob saw a gate into heaven, and when he saw into heaven he was given a revelation of his purpose on earth. The purpose of all true prophetic revelations is so His kingdom will come to earth, and His will be done on earth as it is in heaven. True prophetic revelation will always be practical.

The third point is that the word translated "angel" in the text above is the Hebrew word *mal'ak* (mal-awk'), which *Strong's* defines as: "from an unused root meaning to despatch as a deputy; a messenger; specifically, of God, i.e. an angel (also a prophet, priest or teacher): KJV—ambassador, angel, king, messenger." The point is the messengers that are to ascend and descend upon this ladder are not just angelic beings, but God's messengers, which we are called to be.

The forth point is that the messengers of God are called to ascend and descend upon this ladder. A primary purpose of prophetic revelation is to call the church to rise above the earth and to dwell in the heavenly realm now. Just as the revelation to Jacob spoke of the land he was lying on, the purpose of our entering into the heavenly realm is to bring the blessings and benefits of that realm to earth.

For the next point we need to read John 1:49-51:

Nathanael answered Him, "Rabbi, You are the Son of God; You are the King of Israel."

Jesus answered and said to him, "Because I said to you that I saw you under the fig tree, do you believe? You shall see greater things than these."

And He said to him, "Truly, truly, I say to you, you shall see the heavens opened, and the angels of God ascending and descending on the Son of Man."

Here we see that Jesus is Jacob's ladder. The rungs on the ladder are the progressive revelations of Jesus. When we come to know Him as our Savior we take a step. When we come to know Him as our Lord we take another. When we come to know Him as the Lord above all lords we go higher. When we see Him as the One through whom and for whom all things were made, we take another step, etc.

The purpose of our study is to see our step-by-step progression to spiritual maturity. Understanding Jacob's ladder is the center-piece of our study, and our calling. It is the calling of every Christian, who is called to be a messenger of God, to continually enter into the heavenly realm—where we get our message or blessing for the earth. We do this by increasing our knowledge and understanding of Jesus, who He is and where He now sits—above all rule, authority, and power.

We must become more than comfortable in the heavenly realm; it must be our home—where we are more at home there than we are on this earth. I saw a sign by a church that said, "We are just a waiting room for heaven." That is *not* what we are called to be. We are called to be a gateway to heaven through which people can enter into and begin to experience heaven now! Every time we ascend we will descend with a blessing for the earth. The blessing we come back with is a piece of heaven—evidence of its existence.

In this way, we should be turning every place where we are called—our churches, jobs, and homes, even the places where we shop into an outpost of heaven. The way we do this is the Way, Jesus. Even heaven would not be heaven without Him. The Lord is what makes heaven, heaven. As we ascend by the progressive revelation of who He is, we will see more glory, and we will carry that glory with us. This is the call of Revelation 4:1-2:

> **After these things I looked, and behold, a door standing open in heaven, and the first voice which I had heard, like the sound of a trumpet speaking with me, said, "Come up here, and I will show you what must take place after these things."**
> **Immediately I was in the Spirit; and behold, a throne was standing in heaven, and One sitting on the throne.**

That same door is open for you right now. The Lord is calling us to come up to where He sits. Just as there seems to be no limit to the expanding universe that we can see, neither is there a limit to the one we can only see with the eyes of our heart. He has not limited how far we can go, even to sitting with Him on His throne. What could we possibly have better to do?

You can find additional Scriptures regarding this teaching in Ephesians 1:18-23, and 2:4-7.

Notes:

DAY 15

The Test

We need to understand a crucial matter which is essential if we are to enter into and dwell in the heavenly realm. This is typified by the "manna test," the first test given to Israel after their departure from Egypt. It was so crucial that the Lord said this test was given to see if the people would walk in His ways or not. Likewise for us, this is one of the primary tests that determine if we will walk in the ways of the Lord, or not. We see this in Exodus 16:4, and Deuteronomy 8:16:

> Then the LORD said to Moses, "Behold, I will rain bread from heaven for you; and the people shall go out and gather a day's portion every day, that I may test them, whether or not they will walk in My instruction.
>
> In the wilderness He fed you manna which your fathers did not know, that He might humble you and that He might test you, to do good for you in the end.

As we read in Psalm 78:23-25:

> Yet He commanded the clouds above, and opened the doors of heaven;
> And He rained down manna upon them to eat, and gave them food from heaven.
> Man did eat the bread of angels; He sent them food in abundance.

Manna was bread from heaven. The children of Israel were commanded to eat this bread as both a test, and to humble them. This remains a primary test for the Lord's people to determine if we are going to walk in His ways. It is also a way that we humble ourselves. The test is to see if we will get up first thing each morning and seek fresh bread from heaven. This is also the humility by which we acknowledge that we simply cannot make it a single day, walking uprightly in the way of the Lord, without the heavenly manna that He provides for us.

Of course, as we read in John 6:31-35, Jesus is the Manna from heaven. We must have a fresh encounter with Him, every day, and we must partake of Him every day. We should be more addicted to the Son of God than a junky is for his next fix. We actually are. If a junky does not get his fix he will soon begin to shake. Most of the shaking we go through in life is the result of our not having partaken of Christ, every day. We, too, lose our spiritual strength, our vision, and soon go into spiritual convulsions when we do not partake of Him.

It is also true that "we are what we eat." Just as our physical body can be greatly impacted by what we put into it, so is our spiritual make up. If we are partaking of Christ, we will be changed into His nature. Likewise, if we are partaking of evil spiritual fruit such as gossip, slander, selfish ambition, bitterness, resentment, greed, or unforgiveness, we will begin to manifest the nature of the devil. If we are going to dwell in the heavenly realm, we need to watch what we eat and determine that we are going to seek Manna from heaven, the first thing every day.

We must never forget that His primary purpose is not just having us believe His Word, but having His Word change us. He wants us to be like Him, not merely doing the right things, but doing them for the right reasons—because we love righteousness. That is why He commanded Ezekiel to "eat the scroll" before he was to go and preach (see Ezekiel 3:1-4).

The Lord has provided heavenly bread that we can gather every day. Like the manna He gave to Israel in the wilderness, it cannot be stored, but must be gathered and partaken of fresh each day. As we partake of it and become what we're eating, our lives will also be like fresh bread to others. This will cause all to be drawn to the One who is the true Manna.

DAY 16

The Great Promise

The Lord gave a great promise that Peter quoted from Joel on the Day of Pentecost, which we see in Acts 2:17:

'And it shall be in the last days,' God says, 'That I will pour forth of My Spirit upon all mankind; and your sons and your daughters shall prophesy, and your young men shall see visions, and your old men shall dream dreams.

In the last days these prophetic experiences will become much more frequent because we are going to need them during this time. The gifts of the Spirit are not given just to make our meetings better, or to make our lives more interesting, though they certainly do this. They are given to us because we need them to accomplish the purpose of the Lord in our time.

That His Spirit is poured out upon **"all mankind"** could have literally been translated, "all of the body." (The Greek word translated **"mankind"** in this text is *sarx,* which is defined as "flesh, i.e. the meat of an animal, or the body..."). This is not implying the Lord is going to be pouring out His Spirit on every human being, but He is going to pour out His Spirit on His whole body, the church. At the end, every true believer, regardless of their denominational affiliation, or even their beliefs about the present working of the Holy Spirit, will be empowered by the Holy Spirit.

As the Spirit is poured out on "the whole body" the result will be prophetic revelation such as dreams, visions, and prophecies. This is why it is so crucial that we learn to discern, interpret, and apply them properly. If you have not already started having such experiences, you will, as the prophecies from Joel and Acts make clear.

If we are going to dwell in the heavenly realm we must learn the language of the Spirit, which is very different than human language. With the Lord, the saying "a picture is worth a thousand words" is even more true. The Lord conveys many of His messages to us in this way. These do not just convey facts or commands, but they also reveal His heart and the reasons behind His actions, so we can be in unity with Him.

There are still many who believe that since we have the Scriptures, we have no need for the Lord to speak to us. We certainly do not want to in any way detract from the immeasurable value of the Scriptures. But this kind of argument is not only in conflict with the teaching of the Scriptures from beginning to end, it misses something fundamental in the very relationship between God and men. The church is called to be His bride. How would any bride feel if on her wedding day her bridegroom handed her a book saying, "I wrote this for you so I will not have to speak to you again."

The Scriptures are complete, and are alone the basis for our doctrine. The gift of prophecy is not given to establish doctrine—we have the Scriptures for that. Prophecy is given for revealing the strategic will of the Lord in specific situations. Even those who claim they do not believe the Lord speaks to us in this way will usually say they are in ministry because the Lord spoke to them in some way. However, prophecy is not just about the strategic will of the Lord. The quality of any relationship will be measured by the quality of the communication. Much of what the Lord is saying to His people is simply "love talk," by which He is wooing us closer to Himself.

It is certainly important for us to be solidly established in sound biblical doctrine. It is important for us to know the plan of God, and the strategic will of God for our own life. Even so, there is nothing in our life more important than getting closer to Him, and abiding in Him day-by-day. That is why it is written in Matthew 4:4,

But He (Jesus) answered and said, "It is written, Man shall not live on bread alone, but on every word that proceeds out of the mouth of God."

Note that the Lord did not say we are to live by the words that *proceeded* out of the mouth of God, but by every word that *proceeds,* present tense. It is certainly important we honor all that the Lord has said, but we live by what He is saying presently. Again, this is not just about doctrine or teaching, but about relationship. This is not an either/or choice. We need both to know Him and abide in Him.

DAY 17

Caught Between Heaven and Earth

For today's study we will look at Ezekiel 8:3 for a very important understanding about the prophetic:

> **And He stretched out the form of a hand and caught me by a lock of my head; and the Spirit lifted me up between earth and heaven and brought me in the visions of God to Jerusalem, to the entrance of the north gate of the inner court, where the seat of the idol of jealousy, which provokes to jealousy, was located.**

Here we see that Ezekiel was not caught up into heaven, but between earth and heaven. We call this the "second heaven," or the heavenly realm that Satan now rules as the prince of the powers of the air. If Ezekiel had been caught up into heaven itself he would have seen the New Jerusalem that is pure and spotless, the bride of the Lamb. Instead he saw the tragic state of the temple at that time. My point is that just because we see a vision, regardless of how supernatural it is, even if it is one that the Spirit lifted us up to see, it does not necessarily reveal God's will. It can reveal the present state of things, or even the future. It can also reveal the schemes of the devil rather than the will of God.

There are principles and there are laws. Principles often have exceptions to them. What I am about to share with you is a principle. When we are given a supernatural revelation of something that is bad, it is often given to us so we can prevent it from happening, not so we will prophesy it. We do not want to prophesy the devil's intentions.

For example, if I was shown that someone's marriage was about to break up, I would not prophesy this, but would ask the Lord for words of encouragement about how glorious their marriage can be if they will turn to the Lord and ask for His help. Likewise, if I saw a church that was about to suffer an attack, I probably would ask for words of wisdom to give them that would strengthen them against the attack. I do this because many times, warnings create fear rather than faith. As I said, this is a principle, not a law. There are certainly times to be straightforward with what you see.

The Scriptures are full of examples of how the future can be changed by repentance or intercession. For example, Jonah had a sure revelation that Nineveh was about to be destroyed, and it was true, and from the Lord. However, what Jonah did not count on was Nineveh's repentance. Because of it the Lord changed His mind and did not destroy Nineveh.

Almost every prophecy of judgment should be accompanied by "unless you repent." This is why, when the Lord revealed His intention to destroy Sodom that Abraham felt he could entreat the Lord to spare it if He found just ten righteous men there. The Lord would have then spared it, but He could not find ten.

The reverse is likewise true since almost every promise of God is accompanied by conditions that must be met. Was Moses a false prophet for telling the Israelites in Egypt that the Lord was going to take them to a land flowing with milk and honey, when all but two from that first generation perished in the wilderness? Of course not. It was God's intention to carry all of them to the Promised Land, but they disqualified themselves from fulfilling their calling by following their fears and becoming complainers, rather than having faith in God.

We must recognize the prophecies that come from **"between earth and heaven"** are changeable for either good or bad. This is grace from the Lord. However, there is a realm from which His unchangeable will is revealed. This is rarely experienced by those living on the earth because He is more concerned that we grow in faith, wisdom, and the knowledge of His ways which require faith.

Why does the Lord make these things so ambiguous? So we will grow in humility. He won't allow us to figure some things out because then we would not need Him. Remember, Satan grew in pride and fell. The Lord has so ordained that even the greatest prophets only "see in part" (see I Corinthians 13:9). Therefore, for us to have the whole picture, we must put our little part together with what others are seeing. This will require humility that will also lead to unity, and is why we are also promised concerning the prophets in Isaiah 52:8: **"Thy watchmen shall lift up the voice; with the voice together shall they sing: for they shall see eye to eye, when the LORD shall bring again Zion" (KJV).**

In due time unity will come. Then we will see the whole picture clearly. We will never see His whole plan until we realize how much we need each other.

DAY 18

The Expanse of Heaven

We have been looking at our call to enter into and live in the heavenly realm, now. We addressed Jacob's ladder, and how it represented Christ. He is the Way by which we climb into the heavenly realm. We discussed how the messengers of God are ascending *and* descending upon this ladder. We are called to enter into the heavenly realm, but we are also to descend back to earth with what we receive in the heavenly realm. This is what I want to discuss a little more at this time.

As a jet pilot I used to love flying at the highest altitudes. On a clear winter night above 40,000 feet, you can see from Washington, D.C. to New York. From my cockpit it was a spectacular sight, hundreds of thousands of lights sparkling across what appeared to be just a few feet stretched out below me. I would marvel when I thought of all that was probably going on within my eyesight at that time. As I looked down at this beautiful, seemingly peaceful sight, statistically speaking, there were probably a number of murders being committed, rapes, robberies, tragic accidents, and a multitude of other problems going on. From my position, it was hard to imagine all of that happening. Consider how much more it looks like that from space, or from God's perspective in heaven.

What's my point? C.S. Lewis once wrote that heaven was so much bigger than the earth that if all of the evil ever done in the world were rolled into a ball, and hurled at a mere sparrow in heaven, it would not have enough substance there to even register as a thought! Compared to the universe, the whole earth is like a spec of sand to the ocean. Satan and his hosts have been cast out of heaven and have come with great wrath to the earth. However, the rest of the entire universe obeys the Lord. It is only this tiny, little speck of a planet that has rebelled. All of the evil balanced against the goodness of the Lord throughout the physical universe would be like weighing a single snowflake against the Himalayas.

Heaven is big! Your future is bigger than your greatest thoughts can yet comprehend. Your inheritance cannot even be properly compared with anything known on earth—it is too big! The Lord came to show us how to start thinking from that perspective, His perspective in heaven.

When the Lord decided to multiply the bread, He did not do it for just a few friends. He waited until He had a crowd of 5,000! When He turned the water into wine He did not just make a few bottles—He made about 120 gallons! He was trying to show His disciples how to think big. There was no way that they could exhaust heaven's supply of bread or wine. He could have filled the Sea of Galilee with wine from above and no one in heaven would have missed it. In fact, it probably would not have even been enough to register as a drop there.

We have a Source who will never run out. All of us can draw on heaven's account for a million times more than we already have and it would hardly be enough to even get anyone's attention in heaven. God is big! We are called to reveal how big He is, as well as how wonderful He is. This is one reason why we must learn to ascend into heaven, and come back with a demonstration of heaven. A mustard seed of faith in heaven is greater than a mountain here.

While you are ascending into heaven, look down. The things of this world will grow strangely dim, and strangely small. When I am flying, I can look down on a thousand terrible events and not even see them because they are too small. All of the things that overwhelm our thinking each day would not even be able to register as a thought if we were truly seated with Christ in the heavenly places.

However, as tiny as we are, the Lord chooses to see us and intervene in our lives. As we are seated with Him, we too, will look down, and begin to intervene with the power to do something about what is happening here. That is our calling. To accomplish it, we must put everything in perspective. The perspective of truth is that God is big and all of the problems on earth are small to Him. This is the truth, and the way we will begin to see reality. To see this reality is called F-A-I-T-H.

Some people do not take their problems to God because they actually feel it would be a bother to Him. They just do not realize how big He is. Such thinking is a supreme delusion. All of our problems combined will never amount to enough to register as weight to Him. There is no way we will ever be big enough to bother Him. Just give Him everything. A huge load to us is nothing to Him. When we get this load off of us we will be able to help others with theirs. That's what He wants. That's our other job description—to love one another. With the load off, we will be able to climb the ladder easier, and bring far more of heaven back to the earth. This is what is stated Isaiah in 40:21-29:

> Do you not know? Have you not heard? Has it not been declared to you from the beginning? Have you not understood from the foundations of the earth?
>
> It is He who sits above the vault of the earth, and its inhabitants are like grasshoppers, who stretches out the heavens like a curtain and spreads them out like a tent to dwell in.
>
> He it is who reduces rulers to nothing, who makes the judges of the earth meaningless.
>
> Scarcely have they been planted, scarcely have they been sown, scarcely has their stock taken root in the earth, but He merely blows on them, and they wither, and the storm carries them away like stubble.
>
> "To whom then will you liken Me that I should be his equal?" says the Holy One.
>
> Lift up your eyes on high and see who has created these stars, the One who leads forth their host by number, He calls them all by name; because of the greatness of His might and the strength of His power not one of them is missing.
>
> Why do you say, O Jacob, and assert, O Israel, "My way is hidden from the LORD, and the justice due me escapes the notice of my God"?
>
> Do you not know? Have you not heard? The everlasting God, the LORD, the Creator of the ends of the earth does not become weary or tired. His understanding is inscrutable.
>
> He gives strength to the weary, and to him who lacks might He increases power.

As the Lord explained in John 6:29, "...**This is the work of God, that you believe in Him whom He has sent.**" Basically, this means our whole job description as Christians is to understand how big He is.

<u>Notes:</u>

DAY 19

Heaven in a Mountain

A fundamental calling of Christians is to experience heaven, and bring heaven to earth. The prayer the Lord gave us to pray is for His kingdom to come and His will to be done on earth as it is in heaven. Daniel gave a very specific prophecy about how this would happen when he interpreted Nebuchadnezzar's dream.

This dream is remarkable for its accurate foretelling of the coming great empires of men, which have now been fulfilled just as he foresaw. Now, it is time for the rest of it to be fulfilled—for the little stone to grow into a mountain that fills the whole earth. To understand what the Lord is doing in the earth today it is important to understand this dream, along with Daniel's interpretation, which we will read in brief from Daniel 2:28, 31-45:

> **However, there is a God in heaven who reveals mysteries, and He has made known to King Nebuchadnezzar what will take place in the latter days. This was your dream and the visions in your mind while on your bed.**
>
> **You, O king, were looking and behold, there was a single great statue; that statue, which was large and of extraordinary splendor, was standing in front of you, and its appearance was awesome.**
>
> **The head of that statue was made of fine gold, its breast and its arms of silver, its belly and its thighs of bronze,**
>
> **its legs of iron, its feet partly of iron and partly of clay.**
>
> **You continued looking until a stone was cut out without hands, and it struck the statue on its feet of iron and clay, and crushed them.**
>
> **Then the iron, the clay, the bronze, the silver and the gold were crushed all at the same time, and became like chaff from the summer threshing floors; and the wind carried them away so that not a trace of them was found. But the stone that struck the statue became a great mountain and filled the whole earth.**

This was the dream; now we shall tell its interpretation before the king.

You, O king...are the head of gold.

And after you there will arise another kingdom inferior to you, then another third kingdom of bronze...

Then there will be a fourth kingdom as strong as iron; inasmuch as iron crushes and shatters all things, so, like iron that breaks in pieces, it will crush and break all these in pieces.

And in that you saw the feet and toes, partly of potter's clay and partly of iron, it will be a divided kingdom; but it will have in it the toughness of iron, inasmuch as you saw the iron mixed with common clay...

And in that you saw the iron mixed with common clay, they will combine with one another in the seed of men; but they will not adhere to one another, even as iron does not combine with pottery.

And in the days of those kings the God of heaven will set up a kingdom which will never be destroyed, and that kingdom will not be left for another people; it will crush and put an end to all these kingdoms, but it will itself endure forever.

Inasmuch as you saw that a stone was cut out of the mountain without hands and that it crushed the iron, the bronze, the clay, the silver, and the gold, the great God has made known to the king what will take place in the future; so the dream is true, and its interpretation is trustworthy."

The history of the following empires of men remarkably followed the pattern of this dream. Theologians and historians almost universally agree that these kingdoms were Media Persia, Greece, the Roman Empire, then the Holy Roman Empire, which was represented by feet of iron and clay because it was a mixture of Rome (iron) and the church (clay).

These kingdoms were all much more than just their periods of domain in history. They were humanistic philosophies, doctrines, customs, cultural, and religious influences that were passed down and continue to have an influence on the entire earth. This statue was of a man because it represents the kingdoms of man. As Daniel asserted, in "the latter days" there will be a "little stone" that will strike the feet of this statue and bring it all down.

Here we see that the kingdom of God will begin very small, but even a small stone from heaven can easily overthrow all of the kingdoms, philosophies, doctrines, and religions of men. When we confront such things we often feel compelled to attack the whole statue, but all the Lord does is cast a little stone at their feet and all that man has built in opposition or rebellion to God will collapse.

The stone is Christ, and the mountain is His government, which is **"the kingdom of God."** This speaks of His authority and dominion growing until it fills the earth. This is now taking place. We are called to be a part of it, by taking dominion for the kingdom of God wherever He has placed us. We are called to turn our homes into a piece of heaven. We are called to turn our jobs, schools, places where we shop, everywhere we go, into part of the domain of heaven.

To do this we must understand the kingdom of God will not be established like the kingdoms of men. It will not come with carnal weapons, carnal force, political alliances, or other human means, such as the statue that the king of Babylon saw in his dream. It will come by a love so strong that hatred collapses before it. It will come by a joy so powerful that depression dissipates like fog before the sun. It will come through a peace so profound that fear flees from it. It will come with such patience, kindness, goodness, faithfulness, gentleness, and self-control that all authority and influence based on anything man has tried to build on will not be able to stand before it.

The time will soon be upon us when everything man has tried to build will be seen as the fragile idol it is, and it will come down. Our job is to simply grow in the kingdom of God that is **"...righteousness and peace and joy in the Holy Spirit" (Romans 14:17).** We have a kingdom that cannot be shaken, which is irresistible, and which will prevail. Your purpose for being on the earth is to bring the kingdom of heaven to it. Seal Daniel 2:44 in your heart:

> **And in the days of those kings the God of heaven will set up a kingdom which will never be destroyed, and that kingdom will not be left for another people; it will crush and put an end to all these kingdoms, but it will itself endure forever.**

Notes:

DAY 20

For Heaven's Sake

As we have learned, it is the calling of every Christian to experience heaven now, and to live a life that demonstrates the reality of heaven on this earth. We do that by living in heaven now. It is our calling to bring heaven to every place we go, to our homes, our jobs, where we shop, everywhere.

As we grow spiritually, our home, our heart, and our perspective, should be a heavenly one. The Christian life is supposed to be filled with the bliss of heaven. That bliss is the love of God, the peace of God, the patience of God, and the power of God. As we grow into and begin to demonstrate the reality of heaven, we will become contagious, causing everything we come in contact with to begin looking up.

The characteristics of God are shared with man in the form of the fruit of the Spirit, and the gifts of the Spirit. These are together a demonstration that the Lord has risen, He loves man, and continues to seek our redemption, our restoration, and our glorification—to take on His nature. The gifts of the Spirit are the special, personal, demonstrations of His love and willingness to help us. They are also a touch from another, higher reality.

The power of the gifts of the Spirit cannot be explained or understood from an earthly intelligence, but only from a heavenly one. It is a call to the earthbound so they can live in another reality. There is a glib saying that some people are so heavenly minded that they are not any earthly good. That sounds witty, but the truth is that much of the church is so earthly minded that they are not any good to either heaven or earth.

Christianity is not just another, better philosophy of life. It is another reality and another life altogether. We are called to walk the earth, do good on the earth, and to do it with power that is not of this earth. St. Francis of Assisi was once walking with a priest who was pointing out the splendor of a cathedral they were passing. With a touch of pride the priest remarked, "we can no longer say 'silver and gold have we none,'" to which St. Francis replied, "And neither can we say to the cripple, 'rise up and walk!'"

The true, Christian witness that impacts this world will never come from just having better things on earth. There are a number of beautiful church buildings in our city, a couple of them probably as large and splendid as any in America, but they are dwarfed by the banks and other corporate buildings in the city. The people in our city spend much more time serving the banks and other corporations than they do serving the Lord. However, if a single believer begins to touch and demonstrate the reality, that heaven has authority over all cancer, that believer may live in a cabin, but the world will beat a path to their door.

That the world has better buildings than the church should not bother us. If the church had the largest, most glorious buildings on earth it would not, by itself, result in the salvation of a single soul. One Christian anointed by the Holy Spirit can do more for the kingdom of God than all of the buildings constructed in the name of the Lord combined. This is not to say that buildings cannot be useful to the church, but nothing from or on this earth can ever be compared to the Holy Spirit. The wealth and power that resides within a single Christian by the Holy Spirit is greater than all of the wealth and power found on the whole earth.

The Spirit moving brought forth this glorious creation. The Spirit moving can, and will, recreate the world. Since the Lord delegated authority over the earth to man, He now moves on the earth through men. Because, **"The heavens are the heavens of the LORD; but the earth He has given to the sons of men" (Psalm 115:16)**, the Lord requires the cooperation of men to move on the earth. This is why, even though the Lord knows what we need before we ask Him, He requires that we ask before He moves on the earth. When He demonstrates His kingdom and the powers of heaven to the earth, He does it through men.

The Lord could have parted the Red Sea without Moses, but not without violating His own principles of authority. He could have brought down fire on the prophets of Baal without Elijah, but that is not the way He does things on the earth. He gave authority over the earth to men, which is why even the Son of God, Jesus, continually referred to Himself as the Son of Man. He had to come as a man to retake the authority over the earth that had been lost by man's transgression and subsequent subservience to Satan. That is why, when Satan tempted Jesus he tried to get Him to wrongly use His powers as the Son of God, but Jesus responded to Him with *"Man* does not live by bread alone," etc... God ordained that man should rule over the earth and the coming of His kingdom will, therefore, restore man's authority over the earth, to those who worship and obey Him.

DAY 21

Seeing His Work

Jesus used His heavenly powers, but never to fulfill His own human desires, or to testify of Himself as Satan tried to trick Him into doing. When Jesus used the power of the heavenly realm, it was in obedience to the Father in heaven and as a witness of the Father. Because He gave Himself to be a witness of the Father's love, the Father sent the Spirit to witness of the Son. The power of heaven is never used selfishly. That is why selfish ambition can be found at the root of almost every ministry that falls. If we are going to be trusted with the great power that some will exhibit at the end of this age, we must be resolute not to use power for selfish purposes, or testify of ourselves. This must be our constitution.

Have you ever wondered why many who have the greatest healing ministries seem to always be sick or physically afflicted themselves? The gift of healing they were given was not for themselves, but others. I have also often marveled at how those who seem to have the greatest gifts of prophecy have trouble getting a word for themselves. This is actually for our safety. The Lord has composed things in this way so that we all need each other. This also exposes a root of pride if it gets a grip on us. If we begin to think we have such a great gift that we don't need others, we will remain in need. As it is written in James 4:6, "**...GOD is opposed to the proud, but gives grace to the humble.**" We must therefore remain humble to remain in the grace of God.

If we have truly beheld the wonder of the cross, the glory of His resurrection, and where He now sits, it would be one of the most profane, arrogant acts of a perverted fallen nature to use His power to point to ourselves. When we truly begin to perceive the glories of heaven and the One who rules in heaven, like King David, we wonder why the Lord would even consider man, much less choose to dwell among us.

Even so, this is the message of the kingdom that we have been given to preach on this earth, and the message He will back up with demonstrations

71

of its reality. God loves all of mankind and He is coming to dwell with man for eternity. However, the state of mankind will certainly be elevated far beyond its present condition when His glory is fully revealed. If it were not, His glory would destroy us. He is a consuming fire that will burn up the "wood, hay, and chaff."

We are messengers from another kingdom who have been sent ahead to proclaim the coming of our King who is also "not of this world." We cannot represent a kingdom we do not know. We must know the reality of His kingdom, and live in obedience to it now. Our home must be in heaven. Our dwelling place is with the Lord in the Spirit. We are called to be seated with Him in the heavenly places, to see with His eyes, hear with His ears, and understand with His heart. Before the King returns, there will be a witness and demonstration of the reality of the kingdom of heaven on the earth. This will come through messengers who know and live in the reality of that kingdom now. That is our calling.

To those who will walk in this, there will be a profound sense of the greatness of the One we have been sent to represent. We will not dare to pervert the message by using it for selfish reasons, and we will also be totally devoted to doing His will and not our own. We only have true spiritual authority to the degree we are submitted to the King.

Now, this does not mean we need to hear from heaven to buy a can of beans. The more mature and submissive to Him that we become, the more He will trust us to make decisions. Jesus did not have to get a specific word from the Father to heal every person. He had seen the Father heal the sick, and deliver those who were oppressed of the devil, so He went about doing the same.

In general, whatever we have seen Jesus do in the Scriptures we can do also in His Name. There will be some specific instances where we will need special guidance, but for the most part, we do not need a specific word to do what He has already commanded us to do. Even so, our goal should be to "see Him." As we do see Him, beholding His glory, we will be transformed into His same image, and do the same works He did.

One aspect of His nature that we will certainly bear if we have truly seen Him, is a devotion to glorifying God, not ourselves.

DAY 22

Bringing the Day of God

As we have been studying, it is the calling of every Christian to dwell in the heavenly places with Christ and to bring the blessings of heaven to earth. However, our ultimate goal is more than just bringing the blessings of heaven to earth, but rather to bring the kingdom of heaven to earth. Because a kingdom would not be a kingdom without a king, this means the kingdom will never fully come to earth until the King does. So our true purpose is to bring the King to earth.

In II Peter 3:12 we have a remarkable statement when Peter says that we should be **"looking for and *hastening* the coming of the day of God...."** Since I first read it thirty years ago, this Scripture has caused me to marvel, possibly more than any other. Can we really hasten the coming of the Lord? The answer is "Yes!"

How can we possibly hasten the coming of the day of God? When the church makes herself ready, becoming the glorious bride that she is called to be, the Lord is not going to be able to resist her! The Father will just have to let His Son go to her! Then the King and His queen, who will love with perfect love, will rule over the earth until it has been fully restored from the corruption of the fall. Then it will be delivered back to the Father (see I Corinthians 15:22-28).

As we see in the Song of Solomon, the charms of the bride are likened mostly to fruit and the things that make up a bountiful harvest. That is how we make ourselves ready, growing in the fruit of the Spirit, and bringing in the harvest. The truth is, if we grow in the fruit of the Spirit, it will result in a harvest.

Possibly the main reason why the church has repelled so many people is because of our historic tendency to emphasize doctrine instead of life. Certainly we must love the truth, and want to have sound biblical doctrine, but having the doctrine without the life only makes us hypocrites. The truth is the world has plenty of evidence that very few Christians really believe what they preach because if they really believed it they would live differently.

73

However, of even greater concern than how the church so often repels people, should be our concern about how it repels the Lord! If we were more concerned about why the Lord does not come to our meetings, they would be changed into something that would attract both the Lord and people. When Jesus is lifted up, not just doctrines, and not just buildings, programs, or our own personalities, all people will be drawn to Him.

The key words here are "drawn to Him," not us. If people are being drawn to us, that is only evidence of how far we have fallen from our calling. If the Lord is in the house, there is not a single human being that will be getting our attention! As witnessed on the day Solomon dedicated the temple, when the glory of the Lord fills the house all flesh will flee.

It certainly is not wrong to want to reach people, but when we desire that more than wanting to attract the Lord, people become an idol. Our primary calling is to be so attractive to the Lord that He just cannot stand it any longer—He just has to come for His bride! If we become the church that so attracts the Lord, we will also become something so glorious that people will not only cease to be repelled, but they will marvel and look to the One who has so changed us.

DAY 23

Dressing for Heaven

On Day Twenty-two we looked at the remarkable statement that Peter made when he said we should be **"looking for and *hastening* the coming of the day of God...." (II Peter 3:12).** We discussed how the **"coming of the day of the Lord"** can be hastened by the bride making herself ready (see Revelation 19:7). The Lord will not return until the bride says: **"Come!" (Revelation 22:17).** When the yearning in the bride grows to the point where she can no longer endure without Him, He will be so attracted to her that He will have to come for her. It is this yearning for the Lord that will cause the bride to get ready for Him.

We may think all Christians long for the return of the Lord, but it is more likely very few really do at this time. Of course, as soon as we have a major trial, we tend to want Him to come to get us out of it, but few seem to want Him to return because they love Him so much.

Few Christians would actually admit it, but most actually do not want Him to return any time soon. For some it would mess up their ministry! Others just have it too good in this life. As Paul wrote in II Corinthians 5:6, **"...while we are at home in the body we are absent from the Lord."** If we are too comfortable in the world, if our hearts and homes are not in heaven, we have little incentive for seeking to hasten the coming of the day of God.

It is not wrong for Christians to be devoted to their lives on earth. One of the great mistakes of much of the modern church, which has been devoted to the message of the Lord's return, is their failure to build with strategy and vision for the future of the church on the earth. It is good to have a heart for the work that we have been given to do. The answer is not to think less of these things, but we need to love the Lord and His coming even more. The yearning of the bride, which will hasten the coming of the Lord must be, and will be, a passion for Him above all things.

It is not going to be fear of the times, or even fear of the Lord, that causes the bride to make herself ready. She wants to be without spot or wrinkle because she loves Him so much and wants to be perfect for Him. As John wrote concerning His return in I John 3:3, **"And everyone who has this hope fixed on Him purifies himself, just as He is pure."** When the yearning for the return of the Lord compels the church to make herself ready, she will consequently hasten His return.

There is nothing more contagious on this earth than a person who is getting closer to the Lord. If just one person in every congregation catches this passion for the Lord, the entire worldwide body of Christ would soon be transformed. This will happen at some point, and the conditions are right for it now. The drier the wood the quicker it will catch fire, and much of the body of Christ is in quite a spiritual drought at this time. Only the thirsty will seek a drink, and some are becoming thirsty enough to begin seeking Him, again.

It is good to want the Lord so much that we yearn for the second coming, but why don't we start by yearning for His manifest presence in our congregations? Our families? Our jobs? Jesus said in John 12:32, **"And I, if I be lifted up from the earth, will draw all men to Myself."** Of course, He was talking about the cross here, but the earth and all it contains was made by the Lord, and for Him. Nothing that was created can be fulfilled until it is accomplishing the purpose for which it was created, and that can only be done in union with Him. Even if it is misunderstood by most, there is a deep yearning in every soul for God. When He is lifted up, He attracts.

Lifting up the Lord is much more than just talking about Him. It is also more than acknowledging His lordship and glory—it is seeing Him transcend over all things. It is seeing more of Him than anything else. When I fell in love with my wife, I could not think of anything but her, day and night. That is what we can call "first love," or the way we loved at first. We may think this cannot be maintained in a marriage, but it is possible. However, our union with Christ is supposed to be much greater than our union with anyone on earth, since these earthly relationships are but a type, or model of the relationship we should have with Him.

The fire and passion of our first love with Christ can easily be maintained if we will seek Him. Not only is He perfect, but there is no end to the treasures of wisdom and knowledge in Him. He is forever not only interesting, but intriguing beyond anything ever created. We will never exhaust the wonders and marvels of God Himself. Once we start truly beholding the glories that are in Him, we are ruined for life. We just have to have more and more of Him. The more of Him we have, the more addicted to Him we become. But don't worry—He is a well of living water that will never run dry!

Day 24

Who Makes Who?

There is an important question that many ask which seems appropriate to address here. Does the Lord make us into what we should be, or does the bride "make herself ready?" There is sound biblical teaching that reveals both to be true. When we run into paradoxes like this in Scripture it is because there is truth to both. In fact, many of the historic heresies are the result of Christians embracing a truth without understanding and embracing the counterbalancing truth. These are like those who cannot see that a coin has two different sides and therefore half the coins they see, they believe to be fake.

It is an eternal truth that only the Spirit can begat that which is spirit. We cannot make ourselves into what we should be without Him. However, He will not change us without our desiring it. We must want the things of God badly enough to pursue them, as we are told in Matthew 7:7-8:

Ask, and it shall be given to you; seek, and you shall find; knock, and it shall be opened to you.
For everyone who asks receives, and he who seeks finds, and to him who knocks it shall be opened.

When we are born again we begin coming to God like a newborn. We cry when we need something, and He usually responds quickly. Like an infant, we need affection as well as food, diaper changes, etc. Experiencing the affection of God is the greatest joy and fulfillment that we can know as human beings, but it is hard to receive it if we are hungry. Therefore, the Lord gives us food, as well as affection. Even so, a touch from Him has the drawing power to lift our spirits into realms of glory and beauty that are far beyond the earthly realm.

Many have the false concept that the Father is this rigid, intolerant, holy God of the Old Testament, who would be smiting us right now if Jesus had not come to sacrifice Himself for us. The truth is the Father so loved the world that He gave His Son. The Father loves us and loves to affectionately

77

hold His children. God is Spirit and His touch is not like a physical touch—it is much more than a physical touch could ever be. We need this more than we need the things that so often captivate us. The Father loves us much more than we could ever know. He loves us even when we *are* in sin. In fact, He loves us so much even when we *were* in sin that He gave His own Son to help us out of it.

Just as a father's relationship to his children changes as they mature, so does the Father's relationship with us change as we mature. When my daughters were small children, I could hold them for long periods of time without saying a thing and it seemed to be all they wanted. Now that they are teenagers, they want me to take them out to dinner, and sometimes just sit and talk for a while. In the same way, the Father's love and affection for us is no less when we mature, but the way He shows it is different because He relates more to our maturing state.

When my children were very young their mother and I made almost all the decisions in their lives. Even when they cleaned their room, we would have to point out each thing to do. That's okay for a three year old, but if we had to do that for a sixteen year old, we would have a problem! I do not love my sixteen year old less because I do not give her specific instructions about every little thing, but because I trust her more. I would get very concerned and annoyed if I had to give her the kind of specific instructions when she is sixteen as I did when she was three. Neither is it pleasing to our Father in heaven when we fail to mature.

There is a reason why I went from talking about the way the bride makes herself ready to our relationship to the Father. Many fail to distinguish, or understand how to relate to God the Father and God the Son. I knew the day my girls were born that a day would come for each of them when I would no longer be the main man in their life. For a girl to mature into a woman, there are ways she needs a father, but there is a time when that changes and she needs a husband. Even though her relationship to her father will change even more drastically at that point, it can continue, and even grow deeper and more special. A wise father will consider all along that this change is coming, that it is natural and right, and will try to prepare his daughter for it.

Likewise, we need a special relationship with our Father in heaven for us to be prepared for the marriage of the bride to the Son. The Father loves us and we will always have a relationship with Him. It will grow deeper and richer for all of eternity, but there is a different kind of relationship that we are called to have with the Son. We are now preparing for the marriage, but for all of eternity our relationship to the Son will likewise mature and grow deeper. Both of these relationships are required for us to mature spiritually, thus becoming who we are called to be.

Paul Cain once said, "Spiritual maturity does not come by the passage of time, but by right responses to the dealings of God." This is true. We could say that spiritual maturity can only come by right responses to our relationships to both the Father and the Son.

Great movements have recently been born out of the church's need for the affection and love of the Father. This was timely, and badly needed. However, as we get closer to the end of this age the bride is going to be maturing, and she will start yearning for her Husband. Then she will begin to "make herself ready." That will be the greatest sign of all that we have indeed come to the end of this age and are beginning the great day of the Lord.

Notes:

DAY 25

The Veil

The true gospel of the kingdom is a presentation of the King through His people. We read in II Corinthians 3:18, **"But we all, with unveiled face beholding as in a mirror the glory of the Lord, are being transformed into the same image from glory to glory, just as from the Lord, the Spirit."**

It is by beholding the Lord, and seeing His glory that we are transformed. However, we must do this with an **"unveiled face."** What does this mean? We can behold the glory of the Lord, but if there are veils or things in our lives that can distort what we are seeing, it will distort what we are changed into, so we will present a distorted image of Christ.

One of the primary veils that separate and distort our visions of Him in our time is the love of money. As Paul wrote in I Timothy 6:10, **"For the love of money is the root of all evil: which while some coveted after, they have erred from the faith, and pierced themselves through with many sorrows"** (KJV). I quoted from the King James Version here because some of the modern translations have tried to dilute this text by saying such things as the love of money is the root of all *sorts* of evil. But the original text literally said it is the **"root of all evil."** How can that be?

Money can be one of the ultimate idols of the human heart. An idol wasn't just something that the people worshiped in place of God, but it was what they put their trust in instead of Him. Likewise, money is the primary thing that even Christians tend to put their trust in, instead of God. That is why learning to handle money rightly is fundamental to walking in the kingdom, as we read in Luke 16:11-13:

> **If therefore you have not been faithful in the use of unrighteous mammon, who will entrust the true riches to you?**
> **And if you have not been faithful in the use of that which is another's, who will give you that which is your own?**

"No servant can serve two masters; for either he will hate the one, and love the other, or else he will hold to one, and despise the other. You cannot serve God and mammon."

Money is our least valuable resource in the kingdom. It is a resource, and it does have some value, but it is the least of what we need to effectively represent the kingdom. Much more than money, or anything money can buy, we need the anointing of the Holy Spirit.

We do need to learn to manage money properly, and until we do, we cannot be trusted with the true riches of the kingdom, which are such things as the gifts of the Spirit. What amount of money could possibly be worth one word from God, or a single healing or miracle? One of the primary ways that we rightly handle the financial resources we are entrusted with, is to always give the first fruits to the Lord. It is by being faithful in this that opens the windows of heaven for us as we read in Malachi 3:10:

"Bring the whole tithe into the storehouse, so that there may be food in My house, and test Me now in this," says the LORD of hosts, "if I will not open for you the windows of heaven, and pour out for you a blessing until it overflows."

This is the only place in the Scripture the Lord actually invites us to test Him. I have never met a Christian who has done this who does not have the testimony that the Lord is always faithful. I do not think that I have ever met a Christian who was under constant financial stress who was faithful in tithing. Giving our tithes as first fruits to the Lord does not guarantee we will never have financial challenges, but it does guarantee we will be brought through them.

I have met many Christians who believe tithing was the Law and they, therefore, no longer have to do it. This is not the case, and is a misunderstanding of the New Covenant priesthood, which is the Melchizedek priesthood. Abraham gave tithes to Melchizedek before the Law. As we have studied Jacob's ladder, His commitment to the Lord came immediately after he saw this ladder that reached into heaven. We read this in Genesis 28:16-22, but here I will just quote the last three verses where he makes a sacred vow to the Lord:

Then Jacob made a vow, saying, "If God will be with me and will keep me on this journey that I take, and will give me food to eat and garments to wear,
and I return to my father's house in safety, then the LORD will be my God.

"And this stone, which I have set up as a pillar, will be God's house; and of all that Thou dost give me I will surely give a tenth to Thee."

Both Abraham and Jacob understood the importance of the tithe long before the Law was given. Abraham gave in response to the victory that God gave him, and Jacob committed to it in response to the heavenly vision.

Again, our goal is to bring the blessings of heaven to earth, so the world is touched with the reality of heaven. One of the great witnesses of those who have their Source in heaven is how free they are from the love of money. Those who are free of this can have a lot, or have a little, but it does not have them. When we walk in this freedom, we will also begin to experience the power of heaven and its unlimited resources.

Notes:

DAY 26

Walking with God

One of the shortest, but most remarkable stories in Scripture is found in Genesis 5:22-24:

> **Then Enoch walked with God three hundred years after he became the father of Methuselah, and he had other sons and daughters.**
> **So all the days of Enoch were three hundred and sixty-five years.**
> **And Enoch walked with God; and he was not, for God took him.**

Concerning this we read in Hebrews 11:5:

> **By faith Enoch was taken up so that he should not see death; and he was not found because GOD took him up; for he obtained the witness that before his being taken up he was pleasing to God.**

In the last mention of Enoch in Scripture, but not the least important, we are told in Jude 14-16:

> **And about these also Enoch, in the seventh generation from Adam, prophesied, saying, "Behold, the Lord came with many thousands of His holy ones,**
> **to execute judgment upon all, and to convict all the ungodly of all their ungodly deeds which they have done in an ungodly way, and of all the harsh things which ungodly sinners have spoken against Him."**
> **These are grumblers, finding fault, following after their own lusts; they speak arrogantly, flattering people for the sake of gaining an advantage.**

Enoch's is one of the most enigmatic and important messages in Scripture. As we read in Jude, it is also one of the most important for the last days. The special fact about Enoch is that he walked with God. Adam was still alive when Enoch lived. It is probable that he talked with Adam about what it was like to walk with God in the garden, and his heart was so stirred that he began to yearn for such a relationship with his Maker. One of the great, eternal truths is, if we seek God we will find Him. Enoch found Him. He recovered the most basic call of man that had been lost by the fall—the relationship we are called to have with God. Because of this he was delivered from the consequence of the fall, which is death.

Walking with God remains the ultimate and highest quest of man. When this is truly recovered, we too, will be delivered from the consequences of the fall. Enoch walked with God so closely that the Lord took him directly to heaven. This was a foreshadowing of what has been popularly referred to as "the rapture." As Paul wrote in I Corinthians 15:51-52:

> **Behold, I tell you a mystery; we shall not all sleep, but we shall all be changed,**
>
> **in a moment, in the twinkling of an eye, at the last trumpet; for the trumpet will sound, and the dead will be raised imperishable, and we shall be changed.**

Enoch was but the first fruits of the last day church that will also be caught up without tasting death. There have been many books written about how and why this takes place, and many have speculated about the timing of it, but the reason this happens is the same reason it happened to Enoch. The last day church will walk with God so closely that He will be obliged to bring them into the fullness of His presence, transforming them from the mortal to the eternal in the **"twinkling of an eye."**

I have often heard Christians say that they were trying to decrease so the Lord could increase in their life. This seems noble, but it is not biblical, and is actually the opposite of what John the Baptist said, **"He must increase, but I must decrease" (John 3:30).** If we try to decrease before He increases in our life, we will just be empty, and the void will usually be filled with an evil, religious spirit. **"Enoch walked with God, and he was not...."** When we walk with God, we will decrease because He is increasing in our life.

The Lord did not come just to make our lives better and easier. He did not even come simply to change us—He came to kill us! Even though Enoch did not "taste death" in the natural, his old nature was consumed in God. When it says that **"he was not,"** it means much more than him just disappearing. By walking with God His glory changed him, consuming his fallen nature and replacing it with His nature. The same is our goal—to be dead to sin, dead to our former lusts, dead to this world, but alive unto God.

Even so, if we try to crucify ourselves, the result will be self-righteousness. Our old nature was crucified with Christ on the cross. The rendering of our old nature as dead, so we can experience the resurrection life in Christ, is a process that takes place as we walk with God. We identify with His crucifixion, and therefore His righteousness. We will never be so good that we do not need His life and His righteousness. We are only able to enter into the presence of God because of His blood—His atonement. He will forever be our righteousness. Therefore, it is our goal to be found in Him, to abide in Him so that He might dwell in us.

The more we walk with Him and see Him, the more we are changed by who He is. When we focus on crucifying ourselves we are still focusing on self. We will never be changed by seeing who we are, but by beholding who He is. As we behold Him, we embrace and identify with His cross and His resurrection.

Christ is everything. He is the message and purpose of the whole creation. When we lose ourselves in Him we do not lose, we gain everything to infinity. We are exchanging the worthless and the death for that which is beyond valuation, and a life that cannot be destroyed. We will never make a better transaction.

Your ultimate purpose for being on this earth can be summed up in one thing—you are called to walk with God. Your highest purpose for this day is to walk with Him. If you do, you will also make the greatest transaction that can be made on this earth, exchanging some of the death in you for the indestructible life in Him.

Notes:

DAY 27

You Will Prophesy

Another remarkable characteristic about Enoch is that he is the first one recorded in Scripture to have prophesied (see Jude 14). Prophecy is a definite product of walking with God. When we walk with God, so that we are changed into His image, we will begin to see with His eyes, hear with His ears, and understand with His heart. God is beyond time. He sees from the perspective of eternity. To Him the future is just as clear as the present. Because of this, Enoch, who lived in the days of Adam, was able to look all the way to the end and see the second coming of the Lord with His hosts.

It is fitting that Enoch should prophesy of events all the way at the end of this age, since he is a prophetic model of the church at the end. The church at the end is going to walk with God, prophesy, and be caught up into the heavens to be with Him. That is why we see in Acts 2:17-18:

> **And it shall be in the last days, God says, That I will pour forth of My Spirit upon all mankind; and your sons and your daughters shall prophesy, and your young men shall see visions, and your old men shall dream dreams;**
> **Even upon My bondslaves, both men and women, I will in those days pour forth of My Spirit and they shall prophesy.**

Enoch was the first one after the fall to recover the most important purpose for our creation, to walk with God. And when he did, he could not help but to prophesy. Why is this?

First, prophecy is not just predicting the future, but it is speaking on God's behalf. Man was created to be God's representative on the earth, to speak for Him. Remember, Jesus, the One all things were made through and for, is called "the Word of God." It was by His Word that all things were made, and His Word, His communication, is found in everything that was made. That is why Jon Amos Comenius said "Nature is God's second book." This was a paraphrase of what Paul wrote in the first chapter of Romans, that the Lord is revealed in everything that was made.

God speaks. He made His creation to speak through, and man was the crowning glory of His creation. He made man in His image to represent Him, which includes speaking for Him. That is why it appears that everyone in Scripture who walked with God, also prophesied. If we can recover our basic purpose to walk with God, we will also recover our basic purpose to speak for Him.

This is also your destiny. When you were redeemed it was the first step toward recovering the ultimate purpose that you were created for—to walk with God, and to represent Him on the earth. Because He is the Word, He speaks. We cannot represent Him without speaking for Him. That is why we are told in Ephesians 4:29:

> **Let no unwholesome word proceed from your mouth, but only such a word as is good for edification according to the need of the moment, that it may give grace to those who hear.**

Because Jesus Himself is the Word, words have infinite value. Words have power, for good or evil. Words have changed the world far more than armies or politics. Therefore, if we are walking with God, our goal should be for our words to be His words. As we are told in Proverbs 18:21, **"Death and life are in the power of the tongue, and those who love it will eat its fruit."**

What are the fruit of our words? Do they impart reconciliation, faith, love, joy, peace, and patience—the fruit of His Spirit? Do our words represent what the Lord is saying in that situation? Do they impart grace to those who hear them? If we are walking with God, they will, and we will also speak for Him. As the Word Himself told us in Luke 6:45:

> **The good man out of the good treasure of his heart brings forth what is good; and the evil man out of the evil treasure brings forth what is evil; for his mouth speaks from that which fills his heart.**

Is Jesus the One who fills our heart? If so, we will speak His words.

Nowhere in Scripture does it say that you cannot do what Enoch did. The greatest testimony of the last day church will be that she walked with God, and she "was not," because God took her, so she did not even have to taste death. She did not have to taste death because she died daily to herself by walking with Him every day, taking up her cross daily to sacrifice anything that was required to walk with Him. This is the ultimate quest of man. It is your ultimate quest—to walk with God.

DAY 28

Integrity

Recently, I felt compelled to read the memoirs of the Confederate General Robert E. Lee. He is considered to be one of the greatest military leaders of all time, as well as one of the most truly noble in character to have been produced by this country. In many ways, he demonstrated remarkable graciousness and nobility of character, which actually caused him to be almost as beloved in the North as he was in the South after the Civil War. He was regarded as one of the truly Christian men of his time, yet, there are some profound inconsistencies in his life that I have not yet seen addressed by any of his biographers. These inconsistencies with what he claimed to have believed probably caused the deaths of tens of thousands of people, not to mention the ravaging of a nation. Should we not at least try to understand them?

I am not bringing these issues up to defame Robert E. Lee. He was truly a remarkable leader and person. Even so, I believe the same kind of inconsistencies, which are actually contradictions, are today doing great damage within the church, and within our nation. They will continue to ravage us if we do not understand them.

The inconsistencies in Robert E. Lee's actions are highlighted by two of his writings before the Civil War. In one, he gave what must be considered one of the most articulate, concise, and powerful arguments ever written on the evils of slavery. In the second, he did the same for the potential evils and tragedies that would follow the secession of the Southern states from the Union. Yet, he was the most effective warrior on the side that fought for the very things he obviously believed to be great evils. How could this happen? How was it that so many of our founding fathers, who decried the evils of slavery, owned slaves? How could a man who so decried this as one of the "great evils," fight so valiantly for the right to have slaves?

In Robert E. Lee's case, the contradiction between his stated beliefs and his actions happened because he said he could not take up arms against his native state of Virginia. That may seem like a noble loyalty, but is it noble when that state was fighting to preserve something he believed to be evil? Was it right to be loyal to his state and disloyal to the Union that he had sworn an oath to defend when he was an officer in the United States Army? Many others who fought on the side of the South in the Civil War, also declared themselves to be against slavery, and against secession. How could they fight so hard for the things they did not believe in? How do we?

Could it be the same thing that compels people to fight for their denomination, or other institutions, even when those institutions are in conflict with some of the basic truths of the Scripture, and at times the very nature of Christ? Spurgeon once declared that he could find ten men to die for the Bible for every one who would read it! Could this basic hypocrisy be the cause of the civil wars now raging within the body of Christ?

Loyalty is a good and noble characteristic, but we must never let our loyalty to an institution, to a group (such as fraternal orders), or a person, eclipse our loyalty to the Lord Jesus Himself, or to the principles of truth found in the Scriptures. The basic way we can avoid this is not to make vows of allegiance to any organization or group that could lead to a conflict with our allegiance to the Lord and His truth.

Integrity means "to be whole," consistency between our beliefs and our actions. It is this consistency between the Lord's Word and His actions that is basic to His nature. This should also be basic to the nature of all of His true followers. Is it our nature? Where might the conflicts be in our own lives?

The inability of Robert E. Lee to see the conflict between his proclaimed beliefs and his actions cost untold thousands of young men their lives, since it was his genius that prolonged the war for years beyond what it would have otherwise taken for the Union to prevail. Such a dichotomy in our lives may not be *that* costly, but there is always a cost. We may not know until eternity just how many would otherwise have been able to receive the truth of the gospel, if its messenger's lives reflected its message with more integrity.

DAY 29

The Rock

Because Robert E. Lee esteemed loyalty to his native state of Virginia above some of the basic principles he believed, his misplaced loyalty cost multitudes their lives. Many Christians likewise justify their actions, which are in basic conflict with the Scriptures and the nature of the Lord they claim to serve by esteeming loyalty to their nation, denomination, or other institution, above the basic principles of the faith.

This is not to in any way imply that loyalty to our nation, denomination, or even our company, is wrong. Loyalty is a noble characteristic found in every truly noble soul. However, we must esteem loyalty to our God above all of these or they have become idols. We must always obey God rather than men when there is a conflict between the two, if He is truly our Lord.

Many have probably compromised the basic tenets of our faith in this way because they do not really know the basic principles of the faith, having failed to search the Scriptures for themselves. Every nation that goes to war will try to fan the flames of religious zeal on behalf of their cause. Few things are a greater motivation than religious zeal for the devotion and sacrifice required to win a war. Many are duped for the cause of evil in this way. What can we do about it?

If you are wondering where this is leading, I am actually trying to keep you from taking "the mark of the beast." Many have simplistically thought that it will be easy to refuse the mark because they believe if anyone tries to put it on their forehead or hand, especially a mark that includes 666, they simply will not take it. However, a study of this quickly reveals the probability that this mark is far more subtle. It is not just having truth that will keep us from being deceived, but having a love for the truth, which we read in II Thessalonians 2:8-12:

> **And then that lawless one will be revealed whom the Lord will slay with the breath of His mouth and bring to an end by the appearance of His coming;**

that is, the one whose coming is in accord with the activity of Satan, with all power and signs and false wonders,

and with all the deception of wickedness for those who perish, because they did not receive the love of the truth so as to be saved.

And for this reason God will send upon them a deluding influence so that they might believe what is false,

in order that they all may be judged who did not believe the truth, but took pleasure in wickedness.

Robert E. Lee was a remarkably Christ-like man in his daily life and demeanor. He once got down from his horse to minister to a wounded Union soldier who had just cursed him. Several times his top generals failed to carry out his orders at the most crucial point in several major battles, in two cases probably costing him a decisive victory that could have won the war. Even so, he never publicly berated his subordinates, but took all of the blame upon himself. He once got up early to personally serve a meal to a junior officer that he had misjudged. He refused throughout the war to sleep in anything but a tent, sharing all the same hardships that his soldiers did. While Union soldiers burned fields, farms, and towns throughout the South, when Lee marched through Union territory he severely punished any who damaged the property of his enemies, and he made his generals pay the full price for any provisions they took from farmers.

Lee was so noble and steadfast in his basic character that few generals have ever inspired their men to suffer such hardship, and to fight so hard. With little to eat, marching sometimes hundreds of miles with no shoes, suffering the news of their homes being burned and farms destroyed by ravaging Union soldiers, rarely in history have any fought with more valor against greater odds, or for a worse cause. Hundreds of thousands of these great and noble souls died fighting for wrong because of their loyalty to Lee.

Loyalty is a wonderful and glorious motivator, but if we are loyal to any person or entity more than we are loyal to the Lord Jesus and His truth, we too, will be in jeopardy of fighting for wrong regardless of how noble or valiant we are. In history there have been great spiritual men and women who have led great movements, motivating multitudes to sacrifice and valor for the sake of truth and righteousness. There have also been many with seemingly noble character and courage, who have likewise motivated many to sacrifice and valor for doctrines of demons. Being noble in character is important, but it does not negate the need for a devotion to the truth.

I personally have a great concern for Christians in these times. Too many are like sheep who are possibly being led well now, but it is obvious they could easily be led astray because they lack depth in their own convictions. They have not dug their own well. They have not come to know the Lord's voice, or His ways, for themselves. In John 10:4, we are told that the Lord's sheep follow Him because they know His voice. They know *His* voice, not just the voice of a pastor, teacher, or writer. We each have the responsibility to know His voice for ourselves.

We must each dig our own well. We all must go deeper. We must build our lives on sound biblical truth, established in our own hearts. There was a time when Jesus asked His disciples: **"...Who do people say that the Son of Man is?" (Matthew 16:13).** Of course, men were debating that He was the resurrection of many former prophets and righteous men. Then Jesus asked them who they thought He was. When Peter answered that He was the Christ, the Son of the Living God, the Lord responded with:

> **"Blessed are you, Simon Barjona, because flesh and blood did not reveal this to you, but My Father who is in heaven.**
> **And I also say to you that you are Peter, and upon this rock I will build My church; and the gates of Hades shall not overpower it" (Matthew 16:17-18).**

The Lord was not saying that He was going to build His church upon Peter, as some have asserted. Jesus alone is the foundation of the church, and the rock that we must fasten our foundation to is the revelation from the Father of who Jesus is. It is not enough for us to just believe in who our parents say Jesus is, or even who our pastor says He is. We must have our own revelation from the Father of who Jesus is. We will never be able to cast out demons "by Jesus whom Paul preaches." The Jesus whom Paul preached was true for Paul, and all of Paul's writings are true and accurate for doctrine, but we must still have more than that—we must have our own revelation of Him, and even our own conviction about Paul's writings. We will not get to heaven because we are close to someone who is born again, or is growing in Him—*we* must be born again, and grow up into Him.

Notes:

DAY 30

D-Day

Several years ago Mahesh Chavda gave me the book, *D-Day* by Stephen Ambrose, stating that he thought it contained a message for me. It did. In fact, I think it contains a crucial message for the church in our time.

Even the Soviet dictator, Joseph Stalin, acknowledged that the Allied invasion of Europe on D-Day was one of the most extraordinary human accomplishments in history. The plans were so complex that they required hundreds of units, and tens of thousands of men to be at exactly the right place to accomplish their mission by the designated time. When Winston Churchill viewed the plans, he felt the entire mission was an exercise in insanity. If just one unit failed to meet their objective, it could throw off the entire operation. He knew this kind of complex operation was hardly possible in the best-run small organization, much less an entire army. Not only was such coordination between so many units from the navies, armies, and air forces of different nations, far beyond anything that had been accomplished before, even in war games; but they had to cope with a desperate and powerful enemy who would challenge them at every point. Churchill was sure that it could not be done. Then he looked up and saw the confidence of General Eisenhower, and immediately agreed that they could do it!

After leaving the meeting with Eisenhower, Churchill acknowledged to General Montgomery that the plan was impossible, but he also marveled at how differently he felt every time he looked at Eisenhower. In truth, the entire plan that Eisenhower had put together was far too complex, far beyond the ability of any army on earth to accomplish, and would in fact collapse within in the first twenty minutes of the invasion. Of the hundreds of different units with specific objectives for that day, not more than a few dozen actually accomplished them. Many actually landed on beaches miles from where they were supposed to be. Under the merciless fire of the Germans, it was impossible for them to march down the beach to get to the right places.

The confusion on the beach itself caused a great number of men to get completely separated from their units, with some not being reunited for weeks. From the beginning, the beaches were a caldron of death and chaos. The insanely intricate plan the generals had spent years developing was useless, even before the sun had fully risen. Even so, it worked! The Allies won. How did this happen?

Sergeants and junior officers improvised, making up their own plans as they went. If they couldn't accomplish their own objectives they would take up someone else's, hoping another group would accomplish theirs. They won the day because in the midst of terrible confusion they did not let the confusion prevail. They took initiative and fought with all they had. Nineteen and twenty year-old sergeants and lieutenants boldly made decisions that should have been reserved for generals. Everyone decided to do whatever it took to win and worry about who got the credit or blame later.

Stephen Ambrose wrote that it was not the plan that won that day, and not even the might of the army, but democracy won the Battle of D-Day. Freedom had produced men and women who could think for themselves. Freedom is hard. It is hard to make decisions, and freedom allows many mistakes to be made. These mistakes can cause very hard times, such as the Great Depression these young men and women had grown up in. In the Depression, the government did not have the kind of "safety nets" that we do now. If you did not take initiative, you could very well starve. The hard times had worked in them an ability to survive and take initiative even under the worst of circumstances. One could actually say that the Great Depression was what enabled the Allies to win World War II.

In contrast to the Allied forces, even the German generals could not make a decision without approval from Berlin. If the German officers had the same freedom to react to the circumstances as needed, they could have quickly and easily repelled even the most organized invasion. And the one that hit the beaches on D-Day in such confusion and disorder would have presented an easy task.

Did General Eisenhower know the day would unfold as it did? To some degree he must have. Every soldier who has experienced battle knows that no battle ever unfolds as it is planned. The force that can best cope with the confusion of battle and take decisive action will win. Any general would have known this outrageously complex plan would never unfold the way it was planned, and Eisenhower must have, too. Just as every successful football coach will spend days formulating a brilliant game plan, they usually know they will have to throw it away quickly, since situations on the field rarely unfold according to such neat plans.

What does this have to do with us? As we are told in I John 5:19, **"We know that we are of God, and the whole world lies in the power of the evil one."** We are living in enemy territory. We have been dropped behind enemy lines! We are an invasion force that is here to retake the land. What kind of soldier is the church producing for this invasion? Will they have the faith, resolution, and courage to take initiative when they need to? Or are we producing automatons that have been so conditioned by a weak and intimidated leadership that they cannot function without the approval of others?

As Dr. R.T. Kendall points out in his classic work, *Believing God,* it seems that the only common denominator found with those listed in Hebrews 11 is that they all did something no one had ever done before. Is that not one of the greatest demonstrations of faith, to press beyond the present limits, to take initiative, and be creative? Is that not what Jonathan did when he attacked the Philistine garrison with just an armor bearer? Is that not what David did when he slew Goliath? He was not even in the army yet!

True faith is only experienced when we press beyond our comfort level. Great faith requires that we even step out past others. The greatest faith may be going where no one has gone before, and doing what no one has done before. However, faith is not from trust in ourselves, but in the One whom we know rules over all.

Notes:

DAY 31

Who Are You?

But you are a chosen race, a royal priesthood, a holy nation, a people for God's own possession, that you may proclaim the excellencies of Him who has called you out of darkness into His marvelous light;

for you once were not a people, but now you are the people of God; you had not received mercy, but now you have received mercy (I Peter 2:9-10).

The very first group of people to be called a "cult" were the first century Christians. At that time, it was not considered to be a derogatory comment to be called this because the word "cult" was derived from the word "culture." Christians were so different from other people that they were perceived to be an entirely different culture in the midst of the nations at the time. Of course, the word "cult" has a different meaning that we would not want applied to us today, but even so, Christians should be strikingly distinguishable from all other people.

In the Scripture quoted above, we are first declared to be **"a chosen race."** Have you ever considered that once you became a Christian you became part of another race of people? We are no longer white, black, red, Jew, or Gentile. As Christians we are called to be a different race within the earth that is distinguishable, not by the color of our skin, but by our life and character. Our life and character should be so different and powerful in Christlikeness, that we stand out because of them.

It is more difficult for minorities not to think of themselves first as a red or black man or woman, etc. Wherever there has been a history of racial prejudice, those discriminated against have their racial identity thrust upon them in a much stronger way than majorities. Even so, if our identity is not first as a Christian, we have much maturing to do. If our attraction to fellowship is not first toward other Christians above those with whom we are just racially identified, it is an indication that we are placing our identity in the flesh above our identity in the spirit.

This is not to imply that there should not be some identity and fellowship around one's natural race or culture. However, if our identity is not first as a Christian then something is awry. This is probably something that is askew with most Christians today because we fail to see ourselves as the separate race that we are called to be, the **"chosen race."**

The second identity that we are given in I Peter 2:9 is **"a royal priesthood."** One of the great truths highlighted by the Reformation was the priesthood of all believers that the New Covenant makes clear. How many Christians even think in terms of their priestly calling and duties on a daily basis, or at all? Of those who know this doctrinal truth concerning our priesthood, how many are actually functioning in this calling, which we all have?

Not only are we a priesthood, we are a **"royal"** priesthood. Christians are the true royalty in the earth. We are sons and daughters of the King of kings. We should conduct our lives with the dignity, grace, and integrity of such royalty. We should also understand that a priesthood is first for the purpose of serving the Lord, but also serving all nations, races, and cultures with intercession and ministry. If our identity is truly with the Lord first, this duty as priests should be foremost in our minds above any other earthly duties or professions.

The final description that Peter gives to believers is that we are a holy nation. The Greek word translated "holy" in this text is *hagios* (hag'-ee-os), which is defined as "sacred, pure, morally blameless," as well as "religious, ceremonially, consecrated." Recent studies indicate that there is no longer a moral difference between those who consider themselves born again Christians and non-Christians, when just fifty years ago the difference was striking and profound. What has happened? It is the fulfillment of the Lord's own prophecy concerning the last days in Matthew 24:12, **"And because lawlessness is increased, most people's love will grow cold."**

There is clear evidence that in fact most Christians' love has grown cold, and they are no longer distinguishable by their character, their love for God or one another. Even so, nowhere does it say that those whose love has grown cold cannot be reignited. This too is happening. One of the great revivals that is taking place at this time is the recovery of backslidden and lukewarm Christians.

The Word is also clear that before the end comes there is going to be a church that is pure and spotless. This is one of the primary purposes for restoring prophetic ministry to the church. Just as John the Baptist prepared for the Bridegroom the first time he came, there will be a prophetic ministry that will call God's people to repentance in preparation for His second coming. These messengers will be flames of fire, not to condemn, but to save and reignite the passion of our first love in the hearts of the **"chosen race, the royal priesthood,"** that will actually be a separate, **"holy nation"** on the earth when He comes.

Notes:

DAY 32

Where Are You From?

We have been taking a step-by-step approach to establishing a vision of what we are to grow up into as Christians. We have discussed how we are called to be a **"a chosen race, a royal priesthood, a holy nation" (I Peter 2:9).** We are called to be a separate nation within the nations whose very existence testifies of the excellencies of the King who rules over us. Christians should be strikingly distinguishable from all other people. We are in fact the "alien nation" within the nations, as we are a "new creation" that is vastly different from the Adamic nature of man.

This **"holy nation"** also has a different government. Of course, we honor the governments of the nations that we live in because they too have received their authority from God (see Romans 13:1-6), and they are our hosts. Even so, our main purpose on this earth is to prepare the way for the kingdom that is to come, to serve its interests, not just the interests of the nations of this world. That does not mean that we do not seek to be a blessing to the nations, but we serve another King, Jesus. We must place the interests of His kingdom first in all things.

As we proceed toward the end of this age, the **"holy nation"** will become more distinguishable. It will increasingly become a bright light set on a hill in the midst of darkness. The Christian community will become just that, a community within itself with a powerful and distinct identity. This does not mean that we must live in separate neighborhoods, but that the bond between Christians will grow so strong that they will be recognized as a community of people within the community. We will live by a faith and a purpose other than those that the world lives by.

To further understand just how we are to relate to the nations of this earth, I want to briefly discuss the two different kinds of governments that presently rule this world. Later, we will elaborate on how they are distinguishable from the kingdom of God in their basic functions.

Basically, the present governments of this world can be separated into two kinds, the *lawless* and the *lawful*. The lawless nations may have a strong authoritarian government, such as many of the communist governments. If they have a constitution at all, it does not have any real influence because the true rule is at the whim of those in power. In these nations the courts are not established for the purpose of providing justice, but for enforcing the dictates of those in authority. In contrast to this, the *lawful* nations are those that are established on a constitution that has real strength and a system of justice based on protecting the constitution and the rights of the citizens who live under it.

Generally, the *lawful* governments will be much better than the *lawless*, but both fall far short of the government of the kingdom of God. Even in the most lawful nations, law is an art and not a science. By this I mean it can change because of influences justice under the law. One who has the most persuasive lawyers arguing their case can win, the merit of facts actually having little to do with the outcome of the case.

In nations so devoted to the rule of law, such as the United States, right and wrong is often determined by what we can get away with, not what is right or wrong. Even though this may be the case, these systems will probably provide much more true justice than those under a lawless system. However, there will not be true justice until the Judge returns and establishes His kingdom based on truth.

For further study of these two basic types of earthly governments, I highly recommend the writings of Alexander Solzhenitsyn. He lived under the lawless regimes of communism and then spent years under the lawful (or full-of-law) government of the United States. He saw both as falling short of bringing forth the best and highest purposes of mankind. With the eye of a prophet, Solzhenitsyn's address, "A Warning," to the graduating class of Harvard (which was published on the front pages of newspapers throughout the country in 1976) shook our nation as few critics of our country ever have. This was probably one of the two most powerful prophetic proclamations made to this nation in the twentieth century, with the other being the "I Have A Dream" speech made by Martin Luther King, Jr. (We published Solzhenitsyn's address in *The Morning Star Journal, Volume 3, Number 1.*)

In contrast to the best governments of this world, the kingdom of God is based on the highest moral standard—love. We who live in the kingdom should not be governed by what we can get away with, but by what is right and what is of the greatest benefit to those we are commanded to love. It is true that when the King Himself comes to set up His kingdom on earth,

He will come with a rod of iron to judge the nations, but even His judgment is founded upon His love. God who is love, does not do anything out of resentment or retaliation. This was proven for all time by the cross. Even if He must destroy a nation, it is because love makes it necessary.

This certainly is "tough love," but true love is uncompromising in its standards for the sake of those loved. As Proverbs 13:24 declares, **"He who spares his rod hates his son, but he who loves him disciplines him diligently."** If we do not discipline our children we are not preparing them effectively for the life that they are going to face, and are therefore harming them, not loving them. For this reason, Hebrews 12:6-11 states:

> **For those whom the LORD loves He disciplines, and He scourges every son whom He receives."**
>
> **It is for discipline that you endure; God deals with you as with sons; for what son is there whom his father does not discipline?**
>
> **But if you are without discipline, of which all have become partakers, then you are illegitimate children and not sons.**
>
> **Furthermore, we had earthly fathers to discipline us, and we respected them; shall we not much rather be subject to the Father of spirits, and live?**
>
> **For they disciplined us for a short time as seemed best to them, but He disciplines us for our good, that we may share His holiness.**
>
> **All discipline for the moment seems not to be joyful, but sorrowful; yet to those who have been trained by it, afterwards it yields the peaceful fruit of righteousness.**

In our lives, such discipline in the form of trials we endure, is for the purpose of preparing us for His kingdom. His church must be prepared so we are not only ready for it to come, but also ready to take responsibility and authority with Him when He comes. Everything happening in our lives is training for reigning. Don't waste your trials. They are coming upon you because the King loves you and wants to use you for a glorious purpose. It is by passing these tests that we advance step-by-step into the place of being ready for service to the King.

Notes:

DAY 33

Where Are We Going?

As we have learned, we are "**a chosen race, a royal priesthood, a holy nation" (I Peter 2:9).** We are called to be a separate nation within the nations. We are here to live lives that testify of the excellencies of the King we serve. Those who have been born again into this kingdom are a "new creation," vastly different and superior to the old creation man. We are here to represent the glory and the power of the age to come. We are from the future.

The reason the Lord did not catch us up into heaven immediately after our salvation is because we have a mission on earth. Though we were redeemed from the corruption of the fall and already have eternal life, we are going through the process of renewing our minds and natures into the new creation nature of Christlikeness. His whole creation testifies that the nature of God is practical and systematic.

The Lord also has a practical, systematic plan for the **"restoration of all things."** This plan is basically the same as the process of our personal restoration from the old, fallen nature to revealing the power and glory of resurrection life that was purchased for us at the cross. We are going through this process so we can help lead the rest of fallen creation back into harmony with God.

This restoration process will be completed in the age when we rule and reign with Christ over the earth. This is the time that Peter called **"the period of restoration of all things" (Acts 3:21).** We are called to be forerunners and messengers of the coming kingdom. The power of our message will be directly related to the power of the life that is in us. As the apostle Paul declared in I Corinthians 4:20, **"For the kingdom of God does not consist in words, but in power,"** and the power that we have been given to testify of the coming kingdom is the power of life.

We cannot be witnesses of the Almighty God without power. When we think of power we often think of miracles, but they are only one example of

God's power, not the very essence of it. The essence of God's power is the *life* of God. This is why the author of the book of Hebrews explains that the Lord's priesthood is based on **"the power of an indestructible life"** (see Hebrews 7:14-17). Therefore, our goal is not just knowledge or power, but life.

This life is infinitely more precious than anything we could possess on this earth. Many who have walked in the greatest abundance of true life have actually had very few possessions on earth, just like the Prince of Life Himself. There have also been some who have had great possessions, such as the patriarchs Abraham, Isaac, Jacob, King David, and some of the great Christians in history like Count Zinzendorf. However, in all who have true life, there is an obvious focus on things much higher than the treasures of this earth. Those who had true life may have possessed treasures from time to time, but they were not possessed by them.

Our goal is to live and reveal the power of the life that is in Christ Jesus. We use the Way and Truth to lead people to the life. It is our life that makes true Christians strikingly different from all other people on the face of the earth. Again, we are an "alien nation" within the nations. We are a "new creation" that is vastly different from all other men. The difference is not just in our doctrines and beliefs—the difference is the power of the life that we live. We are from another reality and another time. For the message to be fully given to the world, it must be practically revealed by our lives. The body of Christ will arise in the last days as a demonstration to the world, and even to the principalities and powers, of the power of the life that is in Christ.

DAY 34

The Goal of Life Is Life

As we have considered in our study, our goal is not just knowledge or power, but life. In our pursuit of life we will seek knowledge and the power to authenticate our message, but these are just means to the ultimate goal. The life we seek is the person of Jesus—He is the Life.

The life of God is found first in His nature, and then His works. We do not serve Him because of what He does, but because of who He is. Likewise, our calling is not just to *do*, but to *be*. Our calling is to manifest the life that is in Christ Jesus, which He wants to give to a world that is dead in its sins.

There are basically three stages in the process of attaining this life in fullness:

1) The first stage is *revelation*. This is the revelation of what Jesus accomplished on the cross for us. It includes the glory of our deliverance from our old nature, and the glory of our calling and inheritance in Him.

2) The second stage is *working*. This is the actual working out of this salvation by the renewing of our mind—our very nature, in a way that brings practical deliverance from our old nature and establishes His new nature within us.

3) The third and final stage is *revealing*. This is the revealing through us of the glory of the salvation of God, the nature of the new creation, and the inheritance that we have been given as members of His own household—sons and daughters of God.

We can see these three basic stages of maturity repeated over and over in Scripture. They are seen in Israel's departure from Egypt, the wilderness, and the Promised Land. We see them in the three parts of the Tabernacle of Moses, the temples built by Solomon, and the temple built by the remnant that returned from Babylon. All of these were prophetic outlines pointing us to know Jesus as the Way, the Truth, and the Life.

The first stage is basically self-centered because we are learning all we can gain through Christ. Self-centeredness is not wrong for the immature, and immaturity is not wrong when we are young. Infants are almost totally self-centered because they are in such a helpless state. Like children, we must also learn who we are and what we can do before we can begin to relate to others with maturity. One of the true marks of maturity is that we become less self-centered and more Christ-centered and devoted to helping others.

Though the transitions between these stages in our natural lives are usually gradual, they represent specific periods of time in our spiritual lives. The first stage, *revelation,* is fresh and exciting, but usually quite brief. The second stage, *working,* is hard, but also very exciting and fulfilling, and where we learn, grow, and see the glory of the Lord in a way that starts to change us into His image. We must get through the wilderness to get to the Promised Land. This is where the greatest trials and temptations come upon us to test the life that we have been given, and to prepare us for the authority we will be given in stage three, *revealing.*

Stage two can seem like a place where we know mostly defeat and failure, but that is the wrong perspective. We seldom pass one of God's tests with a perfect score. Often we have to be graded "on a curve" with added grace from God in order for us to pass at all. This can be a hard and often depressing stage of our development, which is generally due to our perspectives. We are growing, and even though we may go in circles at times in order to retake the tests that we failed, it was in the wilderness that God's tabernacle was built, and it is in this stage of our growth that the Lord builds His habitation in our life. It is also through our failures that we learn for certain that He is our salvation and victory. Here our faith in ourselves is reduced and our faith in Him grows. This is the level of truth.

The third stage is when all of the dealings of God are applied and we start to possess our inheritance—which is to live by the power of the resurrection life of Christ. This is where glory is not just revealed to us, but through us. This is the place where we start to fulfill our calling and destiny in Him.

The overwhelming majority of Israelites could only enter the Outer Court of the Tabernacle, a few could enter the Holy Place, but only one could enter the Holy of Holies. Likewise, it seems that very few Christians make it past the first stage of maturity. Many shrink back from the dealings of God that would bring them to a place of Christlikeness. These are the Christians whose faith is an appendage to their life. They may faithfully go to services, but their understanding seldom goes beyond the knowledge of salvation. Much of their life is in fact still in Egypt, bound to this present world.

A few go on into the wilderness and begin the exciting life of truly walking with God day-by-day. The first generation of Israelites died wandering in circles in the wilderness because of their lack of faith. Likewise, today it seems that most Christians still do not get any farther than this stage. Many spend their lives going in circles, enduring the same wilderness trials over and over because of a basic lack of faith in God. Even so, those who get this far usually accomplish much for the Lord and His purposes. They build His dwelling place, and help raise up a generation that will cross over and possess the promises of God.

Just as only the High Priest could enter the Holy of Holies, only One can still enter the highest realm. Therefore, for us to enter we must abide in Him. This means that Galatians 2:20 must be a reality in our lives so we too can say in truth, **"I have been crucified with Christ; and it is no longer I who live, but Christ lives in me; and the life which I now live in the flesh I live by faith in the Son of God, who loved me, and delivered Himself up for me."** This is our ultimate goal, and this is where we go beyond just beholding the works of God to beholding His glory.

Again, our goal is life. We must know the way and the truth, but life is our goal. If we do not have His life we do not really know the way or the truth either. We do not just want to know about salvation, but have His salvation working in our lives. We do not seek truth for the sake of having knowledge, but to have the truth that sets us free from our old nature so that we can walk in the newness of life. The goal of truth is also life. Our goal is not just to know about our inheritance and the glory of the age to come—we are called to *live* in it.

Notes:

DAY 35

Finding Your Place in Life

What was the apostle Paul talking about when he wrote near the end of his life that he did not consider that he had yet attained? Attained what—eternal life? Of course not. He attained eternal life the day he first believed. He was talking about "the high calling of God in Christ Jesus." So what is this "high calling" which the apostle Paul considered he had not yet attained, even after accomplishing so much? Let's consider this from Philippians 3:7-14, which is certainly one of the most challenging texts in Scripture:

> But whatever things were gain to me, those things I have counted as loss for the sake of Christ.
> More than that, I count all things to be loss in view of the surpassing value of knowing Christ Jesus my Lord, for whom I have suffered the loss of all things, and count them but rubbish in order that I may gain Christ,
> and may be found in Him, not having a righteousness of my own derived from the Law, but that which is through faith in Christ, the righteousness which comes from God on the basis of faith,
> that I may know Him, and the power of His resurrection and the fellowship of His sufferings, being conformed to His death;
> in order that I may attain to the resurrection from the dead.
> Not that I have already obtained it or have already become perfect, but I press on in order that I may lay hold of that for which also I was laid hold of by Christ Jesus.
> Brethren, I do not regard myself as having laid hold of it yet; but one thing I do: forgetting what lies behind and reaching forward to what lies ahead,
> I press on toward the goal for the prize of the upward call of God in Christ Jesus.

Does this mean we are not all going to be equal in heaven? That is certainly one thing it means. This is an offense to many, especially those who have been privileged to grow up in democracies where all supposedly have an equal vote on matters. However, the Scriptures are quite clear that there is rank in God's kingdom, and we will not all be equal in it. We are right now determining where we will stand, whether we will rule over one city, five, or ten. It is being determined in this life how close we will sit to Him, who is on His right hand and left. There is an eternal reward that is based on our devotion and service in this life.

Many stumble over this truth and many carry it too far. There is a ditch on either side of the path of life. Nevertheless, the truth that there is a high calling in Christ Jesus that is much more than attaining salvation, is overwhelmingly verified in Scripture. What that calling is and how it is attained is debatable. It is also safe to say that if the apostle Paul did not consider himself to have attained it when writing near the end of his life, possibly the most fruitful life ever lived for the kingdom of God, it is probable that we cannot know in this life if we have attained to this high calling or not. However, we should all be pressing on toward it for as long as we remain on the earth.

Many are repelled by this truth and cannot accept it even though the Scriptures are so clear about it. Rank on earth is usually the result of the ability to selfishly dominate others and climb above them. However, we cannot relate heaven or the age to come on earth to the present way of things on earth. The way that authority and rule is presently established on earth is contrary to the way it is gained in heaven—through sacrifice and selflessness.

True Christianity was founded upon a sacrifice, and the power of God is released through the cross (see I Corinthians 1:18). As the Lord declared in Matthew 16:25, **"For whoever wishes to save his life shall lose it; but whoever loses his life for My sake shall find it."** This is contrary to human wisdom and seems like the ultimate foolishness to those whose hope is in this present world. Even so, the true path to life is death to our selfish ambitions, and death to anything that would rival our obedience to the Lord. Even so, it is the best deal we can ever make on this earth. When we lose our life to Him, we will find true life that eclipses anything this earth can offer.

DAY 36

The Creative Power of Life

The whole creation testifies of the ways of the Lord. One fundamental thing that creation reveals is that He is creative! This seems elementary, maybe even foolish to say, but it is obvious that very few Christians really understand this. One of the great tragedies of church history has been the way the fearful and uncreative have so often dominated church leadership and thereby stifled the church's creativity.

To this day there are powerful forces in the church that reward mediocrity and conformity and penalize any who deviate from their own overly narrow perceptions of God and His truth. We will never rise above the powerlessness and deadness of what Christianity in general has become if we do not rise up with courage to throw off the yokes of this perverted conformity, which the Lord never put on His people. Neither will we rise above this powerlessness and deadness if we do not come into the unity He has called us to.

To be a non-conformist merely for the sake of standing against the pressures of conformity will eventually lead to the deadly trap of lawlessness. Again, there is a ditch on either side of the path of life. As the Lord Jesus declared, **"For the gate is small, and the way is narrow that leads to life, and few are those who find it" (Matthew 7:14).** True creativity is not reactionary; it is not against something—it is *for life*.

Jesus was not a revolutionary because He did what He did in reaction to the Pharisees, but because of who He was. The Pharisees reacted to Jesus the way the legalistically religious will always react to His true creative life when it is revealed in someone. However, lawlessness is just as deadly as legalistic religion. Remember, there is a ditch on either side of the path of life.

Because God "the Creator" made man in His image, the true nature of man is also creative. We will never come into the fullness of who we were created to be until and unless we are creative. However, creativity for the sake of creativity will lead to a fall. Man was also created to walk with God, and true creativity that leads to life can only come out of walking with Him.

Though some of the most stifling pressures that inhibit creativity are now found in the church, every art form and style of music can be traced to the church as its birthplace. Presently, many things that are being birthed by the church, are also being driven out of the church by the timid or legalistically religious, and then captured by the enemy and used for his diabolical purposes. This can and must cease.

However, the church has still been the seedbed for the greatest creativity the world has ever known. It will become even more creative before the end, because a new breed of leader is going to be given to the church with the ability to understand and shepherd the greatest powers of creativity that are about to be released through the church. The Lord really has saved His best wine for last. This ultimate release of creativity will also bring revelation of the Creator like man has never known.

It has been estimated that man only uses about 10 percent of his brain, and the greatest genius probably only uses about 15 percent. What is the other 85 percent used for? It is for perceiving, comprehending, and enjoying God. As regeneration truly works in our lives, our minds will be both renewed and restored. We are assured in Romans 8:11: **"But if the Spirit of him that raised up Jesus from the dead dwell in you, he that raised up Christ from the dead shall also quicken your mortal bodies by his Spirit that dwelleth in you"** (KJV).

The Greek word that is translated **"quicken"** in this verse is *zoopoieo*, which literally means to "vitalize, make alive, or give life to." If we are already made alive in Christ when we are reborn, what is there to give life to? He is giving life to that part of us that has been dead, a great portion of which is our minds. As I Corinthians 2:14-16 explains,

> **But a natural man does not accept the things of the Spirit of God; for they are foolishness to him, and he cannot understand them, because they are spiritually appraised.**
> **But he who is spiritual appraises all things, yet he himself is appraised by no man.**
> **For who has known the mind of the LORD, that he should instruct Him? But we have the mind of Christ.**

In reaction to those who have at times been leaders of the church, but obviously had minds that could only understand from the natural perspective, many Christians react to almost any form of thinking or planning.

This is a most tragic deception. Christians should be the most intellectually brilliant human beings on the planet! We have not only been given a spiritual perspective that transcends the natural, we have been given the mind of Christ!

The Lord is not against us using our minds—He is against us not using them! He wants to awaken the 85 percent of our minds that we are currently not using. As this takes place, Christians will rise to the top in every field of science, art, education, and even government.

So, how do we have our minds renewed and awakened? First, we must understand that Paul did not say *"I"* have the mind of Christ, but *"we"* have the mind of Christ. The Lord has designed the new creation as a great corporate body. Walking with God now means being a part of His body, the church. The dynamic of true church life will help to both renew and awaken our minds. This is stated in such Scriptures as I John 1:7, **"but if we walk in the light as He Himself is in the light, we have fellowship with one another, and the blood of Jesus His Son cleanses us from all sin."** If we are not having fellowship with one another we are not walking in the light.

The church is called first to be a family, not an organization. When the organization begins to eclipse relationships, then we are departing from true church life. That is why institutionalized Christianity has always been the greatest threat to the church becoming what it was created to be—a living body with Christ as its head. When true church life is restored the way that it was intended to be, it will awaken us all to far more than we ever dreamed possible in this life. The Lord is going to be revealed in His people, and together they will be a well from which His living water will flow.

Notes:

DAY 37

The Questions of Life

In 2001, we lost our good friend and co-worker, Dennis Rippy, who died of cancer. Dennis battled cancer about as well as anyone could. In 1999, the doctors gave Dennis a 5 percent chance to make it through the night. Dozens from our congregation in Charlotte rallied, many spending all night in the hospital simply refusing to let Dennis go. A couple of weeks later, Dennis left the hospital.

Then in 2001, this terrible enemy struck Dennis again. The doctors gave him thirty days to live. Again Dennis beat the death sentence. Then suddenly a tumor showed up in his brain. Many on our team were at a conference in Switzerland when we received word that Dennis had been given two days to live. Two weeks later he was still fighting. Even so, it was obvious that he was tired. Finally he slipped away.

In the past we have seen cancer healed with a single prayer. Why couldn't Dennis be healed after receiving more prayer for one person than anyone I know? I realize it is not repetitious prayer that moves God, and I did feel that just about everyone's "faith meter" was a little lower during this last battle. Two nights before he died, I heard an audible voice in my sleep saying that Dennis was tired and he would soon die. I called our team leaders, but I could tell that they too knew this was the end. So now do we just smile and go on with life declaring this a victory for Dennis and God's people because he is much better off now?

I know that Dennis is much better off now. I am sure that he's feeling very sorry for us who are still struggling in this life. The Lord will cause this to work for good for everyone, and there will be an ultimate triumph in it. Even so, I do not believe this is the way that any of God's people are supposed to be taken from the earth. I do not think we can call this a victory. The strength of all that we are comes from walking in truth. The truth is that we lost this one. I am not sure why, but I intend to inquire of the Lord until we know. I am not doing this out of guilt or sorrow, but so we do not keep losing these battles.

As Christians we are called to walk in and demonstrate the resurrection power of the Lord. We are called to walk in authority over cancer, AIDS, and every other form of disease. I know this is something we must mature in, and facing the truth is one way to mature. As Paul Cain recently said, "Christian maturity does not come with the passage of time, but by the right responses to the dealings of God." If we are to mature from Dennis' battle, we must have the right response to it.

I am genuinely happy for Dennis. We can rejoice in his life. Even so, our ministry will feel his loss. He and his wife, Jackie, were our first, and most faithful intercessors. Dennis will be missed, and we intend to use his life as motivation to go higher.

First, our goal is that no one in any of our congregations die as a result of sickness or accident. We then want to grow in authority over disease where no one even gets sick. Then we want to grow in this authority so that when we enter a place, the devils cry out and leave, and sickness will flee from us. We want to go throughout the land destroying the works of the devil, healing the sick, casting out demons, and revealing the power of the kingdom of God and His love for mankind.

John Wimber once told me that he prayed for about a thousand people to be healed before he saw his first healing. Because of his perseverance, he probably saw some of the most spectacular healings since the great healing movement of the 1950s. Even so, John always had questions about why certain ones were not healed. He also never said that anyone was healed until they really were. I felt it was this kind of honesty that made him one of the great men of his time.

Even so, John himself suffered from serious heart problems, and one of his sons died of cancer. I felt this was partly because people had a hard time praying for John, thinking their prayers would not mean as much as John's would for himself, since he had so much more authority in this area. However, even the greatest men and women of God find it much easier to have faith for others than for themselves in many areas, especially healing. For this reason we need each other, and even the most quiet, shy believer, who struggles daily in life can have a prayer that moves God to respond.

John raised up some who are still seeing great victories in healing and deliverance. We must do the same. While we will not call these victories, we can be assured of the ultimate victory. There will never be any doubt as to who wins in the end.

DAY 38

The Answers of Life

We have looked at some of the hard questions of life. It is imperative that we ask them, and ask the only One who can truly answer. We should never think that it is a lack of faith, or a challenge to God's integrity to ask such questions, as long as we do it in the right spirit—which is to get an answer.

I think the most crucial questions need to be asked of God, not men. Men will inevitably give us answers. They may even give us the right answers, but even the best answers from men will never satisfy or impart as much faith as the answers that God gives us directly.

When we take our questions to the Lord, He may answer us through men, a sermon, tape, or book, or the answer could even come from a totally unexpected source—but we will know it is the Lord answering our question. When He answers in the special way that He does, it imparts a rock solid faith in our hearts as we receive His answer. This is actually the rock that the Lord said He would build His church upon, as we see in Matthew 16:13-18, which concludes with **"...upon this rock I will build My church; and the gates of Hades shall not overpower it."**

Many have wrongly interpreted these Scriptures to mean that the Lord was going to build His church upon Peter, but that is not what He meant. The rock that the Lord is building His church upon is the revelation from the Father of who Jesus is. We cannot be converted to the Jesus our parents or pastors know, but we must all have a personal revelation from the Father of who Jesus is. He must be our own King and Savior. That is the Rock the church is built upon. Every truth solidly built upon this foundation in our lives will also come from the Father.

It is good to listen to anointed preaching, read books, and seek to learn from others in the body of Christ. Submitting to the body in this way is a part of the humility required. It is also essential for sustaining us. I once heard an old man say that of the thousands of meals his wife had prepared for him, he could only remember a few as being spectacular, but all of them were used to sustain him. Preaching and teaching do not have to be spectacular to sustain us. We just need a balanced, healthy spiritual diet that keeps us going.

However, if we are going to go beyond being sustained to actually growing spiritually, we need to have the Lord Himself teaching us things. We need to have quests for knowledge that we know He has called us to follow. These are often things that we need to keep privately before the Lord so He can reveal them to us in His special way, and we will know it is from God and not man. In this way, we are not just hearing the words of the Lord, but the Word Himself. Though the words may come through a man, we know they are coming straight from God to us. This is the way Paul the apostle received the gospel that he preached, which is probably also one reason that he had such boldness and confidence in it.

Even so, Paul presented his gospel to the leaders of the church after receiving it for the purpose of confirming it, which is also essential before we present such understanding as teaching in the church. We too need to be digging our own wells, asking the Lord Himself to teach us certain things that may be the deepest questions of our heart. But as Paul modeled, before presenting a new teaching as doctrine, it should be confirmed by the shepherds who He has given to us for the protection of the church.

It is also true that everything the Lord shows us personally will probably have been shown to many others. It is not new revelation that we are seeking, but it is simply the truth taught to us by God Himself. When we receive it from our Father in heaven as Peter did, it becomes a rock in our lives that cannot be stolen from us. Teaching that we receive from men is much more easily eroded by challenges from other men.

This is why in our School of Ministry we sometimes invite guest speakers who we know will teach things that are contrary to our own positions on certain matters. At times we even bring in several different teachers to address a subject when we know their teachings will conflict with each other. We do not do this to confuse our students, but to challenge them to search these issues out, and inquire of the Lord for His position on the matter. We know that any who enter the ministry will be continually challenged by different opinions, and we want the ministers that we send out to know how to go to the Teacher for His answers to the questions that will inevitably arise.

We do not want to waste time "reinventing the wheel" with every doctrine, so it is right to go to trusted teachers and pastors for many of our questions. However, even then we should be seeking to hear the voice of our Teacher.

As we are told in I John 2:27:

> **And as for you, the anointing which you received from Him abides in you, and you have no need for anyone to teach you; but as His anointing teaches you about all things, and is true and is not a lie, and just as it has taught you, you abide in Him.**

Some of the foolish and immature have interpreted this to mean that they should never listen to human teachers, but if that were true why would the Lord appoint teachers in His church, and why was so much attention given to the apostles' teaching? This Scripture is saying that we should only seek teaching from those anointed to do it, and we should recognize the anointing as our Teacher's voice. Even so, take your deepest questions to the Lord and patiently let Him teach you in that special way only He can. His teaching will be an immovable rock in your life that you will also find can shut the gates of hell.

Notes:

DAY 39

The Reason for Power

The end of this age is going to conclude with the ultimate conflict between good and evil, which will be a supernatural conflict. If we are going to be witnesses of the Almighty, we must have power. Paul wrote this concerning his message:

> **And my message and my preaching were not in persuasive words of wisdom, but in demonstration of the Spirit and of power, that your faith should not rest on the wisdom of men, but on the power of God (I Corinthians 2:4-5).**

> **For the kingdom of God does not consist in words, but in power (I Corinthians 4:20).**

Though the conflict is a power conflict, it is not to prove who is stronger. Even the devil knows that God easily wins that battle. The conflict is to prove the power of good over evil, truth over lies, love over selfishness. This is why the discipline required of anyone who would be used by God is so hard. We are called not only to do the right things, but to do them for the right reasons. The Lord does not just want us able to do His works, but He wants us to do them because we are in full agreement with Him.

Motives are crucial because as we read in I Corinthians 13, we can have all knowledge, great prophecy, and even the faith to move mountains, but if we do not have love it does not count! That is why this important chapter on love is placed right in the middle of the greatest exhortation for believers to pursue spiritual gifts.

I have heard many say that we should pursue the Giver and not the gifts, but that is actually contrary to the biblical exhortation. One of the ways in which we pursue the Giver is to pursue spiritual gifts. When Jesus walked the earth He demonstrated His spiritual gifts continually, and if we are going to be used to reveal Him, it must be by more than words—it must be by a demonstration of who He is. When His works are manifested through us and we identify with Him in that way, we are drawn closer to Him.

There are many ways the Lord could have revealed His power. He could have moved mountains, cursed whole forests so that they instantly wilted, or raised up whole forests instantly. He could have preached His sermons standing on water. One of the reasons why the Lord chose healing as a primary way to demonstrate His power is because healing also demonstrates His love.

The main reason the Lord heals is that He does not want people to suffer. He has compassion for the suffering. This is why John G. Lake, who had one of the greatest healing ministries of the twentieth century, would pray for the sick until he felt the compassion of God flow through him for that person. He then knew they were healed. He recognized the healing power of God to be present when he felt His compassion present.

There is not a single case in the Bible where someone came to Jesus for healing or deliverance and was rejected. He healed those who did not even thank Him for it, because love does not require appreciation. Love simply does what it can to help others.

Because every believer is called to be like the Lord and therefore do the works that He did, it should be the goal of every believer to grow in spiritual authority until everyone who comes to them for healing or deliverance is healed and delivered. To do this we must grow in faith, but even more importantly, we must grow in love. We see in Galatians 5:6 that faith works by love. And we read in I Timothy 1:5, **"But the goal of our instruction is love from a pure heart and a good conscience and a sincere faith,"** and in I Corinthians 16:14, **"Let all that you do be done in love."**

How would our day be different if we did everything today out of love? If we would begin to live this way, not only would our own lives be infinitely richer, power would also start to flow through us. Love releases God's power because love is the reason for the demonstration of His power. Even so, we do not seek love so we can have power, but we need to seek power so we can demonstrate His love.

I have settled in my own heart by the Scriptures that the Lord does want to heal every person who comes to Him for healing, without exception. He wants to heal even if a person does not have perfect motives, or even good motives. He will heal even those who do not intend to serve Him, and will not require someone to give their life to Him before we pray for them to be healed, in accordance to the exhortation of Romans 2:4, **"Or do you think lightly of the riches of His kindness and forbearance and patience, not knowing that the kindness of God leads you to repentance?"** I think those who are pressured into giving their lives to Jesus so that they can be healed usually backslide quickly, but if they are touched by the kindness of the Lord, it will usually work to bring them to true repentance. Even if it doesn't, the Lord simply loves all people and He will cause His sun to shine on the just and the unjust.

The reason so many people do not get healed is possibly because we complicate it too much, and try to require things for God's grace that He does not require. I believe that John G. Lake probably understood God's healing power best—it is the Lord's compassion for us, period.

My prayer for you is II Thessalonians 1:11-12:

> **To this end also we pray for you always that our God may count you worthy of your calling, and fulfill every desire for goodness and the work of faith with power;**
> **in order that the name of our Lord Jesus may be glorified in you, and you in Him, according to the grace of our God and the Lord Jesus Christ.**

Notes:

DAY 40

Growing Daily

When a child is born, he or she will grow very fast for the first few years of their life. Then they will have plateaus where growth slows. They will also experience "growth spurts," during which time the child's appetite will tend to grow, causing them to shoot up two or three inches in short periods of time. These spurts can be painful, stretching the muscles causing what is known as "growing pains." Even so, as long as they are having them, they are continuing to grow. Spiritual growth is similar to this.

Christians go through the same process after they are born again. The first few years of our new spiritual lives we tend to grow dramatically, and begin exhibiting our unique spiritual personalities. Then we usually have times of leveling off a bit. From that time on, spiritual growth spurts occur causing much growth in short periods of time. Like natural growth spurts, spiritual growth spurts can also be painful because they are stretching us. But it is through such stretching that we remain new wineskins, which are able to hold the new wine that the Lord wants to give us. We should learn to recognize these spurts, and appreciate them as needed because it is by them that we know we are still growing.

In the natural, once we stop growing we start the process of dying. Aging is the process of dying. First we begin to realize that our muscles start getting tired more quickly. Then we start getting a bit sore with exercise. This causes us to get weaker as we tend to resist difficult and painful exercises, which then causes atrophy to the muscles. Then our eyes start to grow dim, and so on. We can fight this process, but at some point it is going to win.

To date I have never met anyone who enjoys aging, but it is presently a part of life that most learn to adjust to. You can learn to enjoy and prosper in the later stages of life. However, spiritually we should never begin this process of dying, but continue growing. We should continue gaining spiritual strength and vision for as long as we are on the earth because there is no limit to how much we can grow spiritually. Even so, if you stop growing, you will start dying spiritually. If you are not taking new ground in the spirit, you are losing it.

As we have read in Exodus 16:4, **"Then the LORD said to Moses, 'Behold, I will rain bread from heaven for you; and the people shall go out and gather a day's portion every day, that I may test them, whether or not they will walk in My instruction.'"** I believe this remains a test for the people of God, which determines whether they will walk in the Lord's instruction or not. This is the test of whether we will get up first thing every day and seek fresh "manna" from heaven. This fresh daily word from heaven will help keep us fresh spiritually. When we stop gathering it every day, we will start to grow stale and often start to deteriorate spiritually.

This daily "manna," or a daily word from heaven, can help sustain us and keep us in a fresh state spiritually, but we need more than this to actually grow spiritually. Growth requires more than what is needed to just sustain us. This is why a child's appetite will tend to increase quite dramatically when they are going through a growth spurt. We need the fresh manna from God, but we also need the meat of the Word. We will not grow unless we are pursuing more and more depth of understanding, and more increase in our vision. As I Corinthians 2:10 states, **"For to us God revealed them through the Spirit; for the Spirit searches all things, even the depths of God."** The Spirit also wants to move in us to search the depths of God.

Psalm 103:7 says, **"He made known His ways to Moses, His acts to the sons of Israel."** Many are content to see the Lord's acts. They will run to and fro to observe them. This is not bad, as it is never a bad thing to want to observe the deeds of God, but we must want more than just seeing His acts, we must desire to know His ways if we are going to grow to maturity.

If the knowledge we are finding does not stretch us a bit then we are probably not growing as we could. Many only pursue the knowledge that already agrees with their beliefs. This is an old wineskin mentality. This is not the way to grow or the way to truth. We must pursue knowledge for the sake of it being true, whether it agrees with our present beliefs about a matter or not. What man on the earth, or who has ever walked the earth with the exception of Jesus, has ever fully known the ways of God? So there is always room for us to grow in knowledge. Even so, our growing in knowledge, even the knowledge of His ways, should not be our ultimate goal. Our goal is to see the glory of His ways so that we are changed into His likeness.

DAY 41

Knowing and Believing

I have been privileged to travel widely throughout the body of Christ, and exposed to almost every kind of major Christian denomination or movement. Presently, many of these groups are in conflict with each other, and some always seem to drift into serious delusions. However, even in its present state I marvel at the brilliance of the church. She is, without question, the greatest creation on earth. Even so, her true greatness is yet to be realized. What could be more wonderful, or more of an honor, than helping to prepare her to be the witness of the unfathomable wisdom of God that she is called to be for all ages to come?

Having begun as the most powerful religious and social force the world has ever known, the church fell into extreme spiritual poverty during the time that it became the most powerful political force in the world. Correction, reform, and maturity has now continued for centuries. The church has proven overall to be a wineskin that can expand to receive increasingly pure new wine.

Certainly there is still a long way to go before the church attains her prophesied maturity of not having spot or wrinkle, to be known for her love, and to be clothed in the glory of God. Those without a historical perspective may have a hard time seeing much progress toward this end, but it is certainly being made. Much of the old is presently experiencing renewal, and there are great new movements constantly pouring new transfusions of life into the universal church. These are certainly wonderful times to be alive and to serve in the household of faith.

From the historical perspective it is also apparent that the Lord did use His church even in her worst condition to speak to every age. The Lord has never required one to be perfect before being used, and He has never required His church to be perfect before using her. We do not get perfected in order to get close to God, or to be used by Him, but we get perfected by getting close to Him and being used by Him. In fact, as He demonstrated with Peter on the Day of Pentecost, He seems to delight in using us in a great way right after a major failure. Like a loving parent with a child, He is always quick to pick us up when we fall, and encourage us to keep going.

It is quite revealing that the Lord sent out His disciples to preach the kingdom, heal the sick, and cast out devils before He even taught them to pray! I am not implying that it is supposed to be this way for us, but I do think that we need to re-examine many of our basic concepts of Christian maturity. Many of those who claim to have the deepest understanding of God and His ways are the least used by Him. Why?

The apostle Paul warned that "knowledge puffs up," and it does seem that many who seek deeper knowledge fall to the pride that disqualifies them from being useful to the Master. However, before we completely write off those who are great with knowledge, let us consider that Paul himself was an exception to this pattern. Even so, he had to be struck blind in the natural before he could see in the Spirit.

In Matthew 22:29 Jesus said, **"...Ye do err, not knowing the scriptures, nor the power of God"** (KJV). This seems to still be true. Those who tend to know the Scriptures err because they do not know the power, and those who know the power err because they do not know the Scriptures. We will continue to fall to error until we know both.

I once asked the head of one of the most successful insurance companies how much training his agents needed to sell their products. I was surprised when he answered that "over-education" was the greatest threat to an agent's success. He himself did not understand why, but they had very solid data indicating that those who were prone to want to know too much before they got started were inevitably the least successful. He said it was the ones you couldn't hold back to sit in a classroom for very long that were always the best. He lamented over the fact that they had such great products that they wanted them to be understood, but he said it was simply a fact that enthusiasm sells ten products for every one that is sold by knowledge.

It is an interesting fact that believers who lead others to the Lord will lead more than 90 percent of them to faith during the first two years after they themselves have been born again. Very few Christians lead others to the Lord after they have been a believer for more than two years. The reverse should be true. As we mature and grow in the knowledge of the Lord's ways, and as we walk more and more in the light, we should lead more and more out of the darkness. Why does knowledge, or even Christian maturity, seem to have this very negative effect?

The first is obviously what Paul warned about, that knowledge can lead to pride. It is rare to meet someone who is devoted to deeper knowledge who is not correspondingly prideful and delusional. It is also rare to meet someone who has great knowledge that also has the substance of that knowledge in their life. This should not be.

When I was a flight instructor the most difficult and dangerous students were those who had studied the training manual so much that they thought they knew how to fly. Reading the manual and flying the airplane are quite different matters. I would rather try to teach someone who thought he or she was a great pilot because they stayed in a Holiday Inn Express, than those who are overly devoted to knowledge without experience.

Yet, it is also true that the Lord lamented in Hosea 4:6, **"My people are destroyed for lack of knowledge. Because you have rejected knowledge, I also will reject you from being My priest...."** As we have mentioned, there is a ditch on either side of the path of life and few seem to be able to stay on the path that is between them.

I love the company of those who love knowledge and are always seeking more understanding of the Lord and His ways. I also love the company of those whose faith is effective and are walking as the Lord walked, healing the sick, casting out demons, and shining light into the darkness to set free those who are bound. These should all be in the same group but presently they rarely are. This must change if we are going to attain what we are called to. We must learn to combine growing in understanding and walking in faith, which are both required to do His work.

Notes:

DAY 42

Speak to the Mountain

One of the great encouragements I have had concerning the potential of the church in our time is meeting the people who attend our conferences. Because they represent many different denominations, and we have had representatives from up to fifty different nations present, we get a pretty good sampling of the body of Christ. I marvel at some of the most mature believers, most of whom have been in Christ for many years, who will humble themselves to be taught by some of our young prophetic people. This combination of maturity, wisdom, and humility is the formula for a spiritual critical mass. That is the formula for a spiritual nuclear explosion of extraordinary power.

I personally believe that right now the church possibly has the greatest body of believers who have ever lived. I also think that overall at this time we may have in the body of Christ some of the greatest shepherds and leaders ever. If we can continue to mature, go higher and higher, while at the same time becoming more humble and teachable, there is no limit to what we may yet attain in our generation.

One of the primary words that I have been hearing from the Lord lately is a call to walk in "the power of the age to come." If this is the time for that power to be released, we are near the beginning of the last day ministry in which the most extraordinary works of all will be released.

The "power of the age to come" is walking in the power of the Lord Jesus ruling upon the earth. Before the end of this age the entire earth will hear the gospel of His kingdom, as the Lord declared in Matthew 24:14, **"And this gospel of the kingdom shall be preached in the whole world for a witness to all the nations, and then the end shall come."** This gospel will not just go out in words. As the apostle Paul stated in I Corinthians 2:4-5, 4:20:

> **And my message and my preaching were not in persuasive words of wisdom, but in demonstration of the Spirit and of power,**

that your faith should not rest on the wisdom of men, but on the power of God.

For the kingdom of God does not consist in words, but in power.

We cannot be witnesses of the Almighty God without power. At the end, when the greatest darkness is covering the earth, the greatest power and glory of the Lord will be poured out upon His people (see Isaiah 60:1-2). The power that I saw coming at our Harvest Conference in 2001 was the power to move mountains.

This does not mean we are going to go forth and start rearranging the Appalachian Mountains, but that we will be given authority to move even the greatest obstacles out of our way. This is the Word of the Lord that was given in Zechariah 4:6-7:

> **Then he answered and said to me, "This is the word of the LORD to Zerubbabel saying, 'Not by might nor by power, but by My Spirit,' says the LORD of hosts.**
> **'What are you, O great mountain? Before Zerubbabel you will become a plain; and he will bring forth the top stone with shouts of "Grace, grace to it!"'"**

The time is coming when some will move literal mountains. However, the one that Zerubbabel was standing before is the one that the church is now standing before—it is the mountain of rubble, the remains of God's temple that has been lying in waste since His people were carried into bondage. There is a remnant that is returning to rebuild His dwelling place on the earth, and they will face the rubble that Christianity has become throughout much of the earth. They too will move this mountain with shouts of **"Grace, grace to it!"**

What has seemed to many to be the impossible task of restoring true apostolic Christianity to the earth is possibly becoming a reality. However, as the Lord told Zerubbabel, it will not be by might or power, but by His Spirit. It will not come through human strategies or good management principles. It will happen with the power of the age to come by demonstrating the authority of the King over all authority, power, and dominion.

Just as He also promised this remnant concerning the restored temple in Haggai 2:9, **"The latter glory of this house will be greater than the former,' says the LORD of hosts, 'and in this place I shall give peace."** We know that before the end the church will be restored to its apostolic glory

138

and power, and that the presence of the Lord will dwell in her. The glory of the Lord will then so fill His temple that no flesh will be able to stand to minister there. Why not us? Why not now?

We may now look at our lives and think that there are too many obstacles—just too many mountains to overcome. It does not matter how big the obstacles are, the Lord is about to release His power to turn every one of them into a plain before us. Start now by declaring to the mountains in your life—"Grace, grace, mountain be gone!" Say to relational problems, "Grace, grace, mountain become a plain!" Say to the obstacles at home, work, and church, "mountain be removed!" Say to fear, say to lust, say to debt, "Grace, grace, mountain be gone!" It does not matter how big they are—before Him they are small! With the power of the Lord that He has entrusted to us by His Holy Spirit, there is no problem too big or barrier that He cannot move. Believe it.

Notes:

DAY 43

The Power of Peace

Before the Lord ascended He gave a wonderful promise, as we read in Acts 1:8: **"but you shall receive power when the Holy Spirit has come upon you; and you shall be My witnesses both in Jerusalem, and in all Judea and Samaria, and even to the remotest part of the earth."**

The enemy of our soul uses fear to keep people in bondage just as the Lord uses faith to set us free. By ratcheting up terrorism the enemy is boldly trying to get the whole world under the control of fear, to have us make decisions and take actions because of fear. If he can succeed, there will be even more division sown between nations and people groups, and more death released in the world because of it. The counter power to this is the peace of God. The peace of God is one of the primary powers of the age to come. That age is going to be ruled by the Prince of Peace from Jerusalem, which means the "city of peace."

Just as Jerusalem is today one of the most violent, strife filled, and fought over cities in the world, it is a barometer of the present condition of humanity. However, Christians have been given a hope which is greater than any other philosophy or religion in the world. A new age is coming that is much greater than any utopia that the New Age Movement has promoted. Jesus is coming back to rule over the world which will again know such peace that even the lions and lambs will lie down together. It is our calling and destiny to live in that peace now.

The peace of God is the linchpin fruit of the Spirit that holds the others together. That is why almost every attack of the enemy is designed to steal our peace first. Satan knows if he can rob us of our peace we will quickly lose our patience, love, faith, and so on. That is why we are told in Philippians 4:7, **"And the peace of God, which surpasses all comprehension, shall guard your hearts and your minds in Christ Jesus."** As long as we abide in the peace of God, our hearts and minds will remain in Christ Jesus.

Because we are experiencing a worldwide assault on our peace, we must strengthen our resolve not only to maintain the peace of God in our hearts, but also to grow in peace and spread it around the world. Every time we are assaulted by circumstances that would cause us to fear and worry, if we determine not to submit to fear or worry, but rather trust in the Lord, we will grow in peace. We spread it every time we abide in the unshakable peace of God as we go forth into the world that is in such turmoil.

We can walk in the power of the age to come now by abiding in the One who is going to rule in the age to come. This is how we become His witnesses, not just by our words about the kingdom, but also by living lives that demonstrate the kingdom. As we are reminded in Hebrews 12:28, **"Therefore, since we receive a kingdom which cannot be shaken, let us show gratitude, by which we may offer to God an acceptable service with reverence and awe."**

What is this acceptable service? It is obedience to the King. This we can only know as we abide in Him day-by-day. If we know we are doing His will, and living in obedience to Him, we will have an unshakable confidence and boldness in this life that is tempered with His love and peace. If we are abiding in the King of kings who sits above all rule, authority, and dominion, who causes all things to work together for good for those who love Him and are called according to His purpose, we will live in an unshakable peace.

As we are told in Romans 8:6, **"For the mind set on the flesh is death, but the mind set on the Spirit is life and peace."** A key to abiding in the peace of God is having our mind set on the Spirit, not the flesh. As we are told in Romans 14:17-19:

> **For the kingdom of God is not eating and drinking, but righteousness and peace and joy in the Holy Spirit.**
> **For he who in this way serves Christ is acceptable to God and approved by men.**
> **So then let us pursue the things which make for peace and the building up of one another.**

The kingdom of God is righteousness, peace, and joy, and they are found in that order. When we walk in righteousness, which is to be right with God and obeying Him, we find peace. When we find the true peace of God, it releases a joy that is beyond any other that we can know in this world. For this reason, we should pursue the things that make for peace, and to build up one another in them. We should seek to sow peace everywhere we go. Determine that you are not going to let fear or terror overtake your office or job place, but that you are going to make it a fortress for the peace of God.

If we are abiding in the Lord, **"...the God of peace will soon crush Satan under your feet" (Romans 16:20).** One of the reasons the enemy seeks to steal our peace first is because he knows if we walk in the peace of God it will crush him in every way that he tries to manifest himself. The key to our victory is walking in the peace of God. When we walk in the peace of God, we are walking in a fundamental power of the age to come, and we bear witnesses of that power. Don't let anything steal your peace.

Notes:

DAY 44

Power for the Right Reasons

As we are told in I Timothy 1:5, **"But the goal of our instruction is love from a pure heart and a good conscience and a sincere faith."** We have discussed our need for power to be witnesses of the God who is all-powerful. We must also understand that God is love and we cannot be His witnesses without love. Our primary goal in life should be the fruit of the Spirit, and power. The power of God is the demonstration of His love.

The Lord did not heal people to reveal His power, but to demonstrate the power of His love for them. If He had wanted to demonstrate His power He could have done much greater things, like moving mountains, or parting seas like Moses. He could have stopped the sun like Joshua, or even written His name across the sky with stars. He used His power for the sake of love. He healed people because He loved them, and He did not want them to be sick. He healed because healing, redemption, and restoration is His nature, because love is His nature.

As we have discussed, we are the Lord's body on the earth. He wants to do His works through His people. He does not just want to use us as He might an inanimate object, but He wants us to be in unity with Him. He wants us to have both His mind and His heart. He wants us to feel what He feels for people. Like John G. Lake, it is wisdom for us to seek to feel what He feels for people when we pray for them.

The Lord did some of His greatest miracles, like walking on the water, before only a handful of people. He could have preached His sermons standing on a lake, but He didn't. When He performed miracles it was not for the purpose of getting people's attention. He did it out of obedience to the Father. Over and over we read that He was moved by compassion because that is what the Father was feeling. We too must learn to be moved by what moves God. There is something in us that will want to do the greatest miracles in front of the most people, but when we are mature, just watching the Lord help others will be our reward.

Some of the greatest demonstrations of power are not found in merely healing people, but in keeping them well. Certainly this does not give as much of a "witness" to His power, but it is just as much a demonstration of His power, and maybe an even greater demonstration of His love. The protection of God is no less a miracle. Let us see and acknowledge His works in all things, knowing that **"Every good thing bestowed and every perfect gift is from above, coming down from the Father of lights, with whom there is no variation, or shifting shadow" (James 1:17).**

It seems that a new wave of power is now being released through the church. Spectacular miracles are taking place. This will increase in waves until His people are walking in all of the works that He did, and even greater works, just as He promised. However, let us settle in our hearts now that we are going to pursue love. As we are told in I Corinthians 13, we can have the faith to move mountains, have the greatest gifts of prophecy, and even die a martyr, but if we do not have love it will not count!

God is all-powerful, but He is also love. As we see His power growing in His church let us also be sure that our love is growing. It is not an either/or situation. We are encouraged to earnestly desire spiritual gifts as well as to pursue love. We must do both. We pursue His gifts in order to demonstrate His love. The power of love is the greatest power of all.

Previously we discussed how we are called to sow peace everywhere we go. We should be building impregnable fortresses of the peace of God in our homes, jobs, places where we shop, and so on. By doing this we are extending the kingdom of God. Now let us join this with the love of God. Peace is not being moved by fear or agitations—love is being moved by compassion. Peace builds a foundation for the work of God, but love does the work.

DAY 45

Serving the King

There are some teachings in the Bible that are hard to understand, and others that are hard to live by. However, the Lord gave us a mandate that does not allow us to pick and choose which teachings we want to accept and which ones we do not. As we read in Matthew 28:18-20:

> **And Jesus came up and spoke to them, saying, "All authority has been given to Me in heaven and on earth.**
> **"Go therefore and make disciples of all the nations, baptizing them in the name of the Father and the Son and the Holy Spirit,**
> **teaching them to observe all that I commanded you; and lo, I am with you always, even to the end of the age."**

To summarize, because He has been given *"all authority,"* we are to go and make disciples of *all* nations, by teaching them to observe *all* that He commanded. This is an all-inclusive mandate. It is the Lord's obvious intention to return all of creation to His ultimate authority.

However, we are not fit to go forth with this great commission unless He is the Lord of our entire life. This is not to imply that we must be perfect before He can use us, but how can we go forth teaching others to observe all that He commanded, if we are not devoted to such obedience? Do we live our lives under His authority? Or do we like to teach about it while continuing to live for ourselves, doing our own thing? Do we even know *all* that He commanded?

This is obviously a tall order, and the first thought that would come to many of us might be, how could we even begin to find the time to accomplish *all* of this? We should first ask ourselves, what do we do that is more important than this? If we are in fact redeemed, we have been bought with a price and we no longer belong to ourselves, but to Him. Those who have been redeemed are no longer to live for themselves, but for the One who redeemed them.

First, we must come to know all that He has commanded before we can go forth and do it. Did you know if you read just two chapters of the New Testament every day, you will read through it entirely three and one half times a year? If you have been a Christian for twenty years and began reading just two chapters in the New Testament every day, you would have read it through seventy times! You would not only know very well all that the Lord commanded, but His Word would be flowing through you continually, washing and transforming you by the renewing of your mind.

If you added reading just two chapters of the Old Testament every day, you would read it entirely through every year. This would also give you an overview of the entire unfolding plan of God every year. As we are told in I Corinthians 10:11, concerning the events of the Old Testament, **"Now these things happened to them as an example, and they were written for our instruction, upon whom the ends of the ages have come."** They were written for our instruction, so we must need them.

Now we may think this is a lot of reading, and yes it could take thirty to forty-five minutes every day. That seems like a lot, but how much time did you spend watching television today? The average American spends between two and four hours a day in front of the television. Is that more important than learning what the King expects of us?

What would happen if we spent just as much time feeding our soul as we do our flesh every day? Do we give the King of kings even less time than we do our stomachs? The lives of most Christians would be radically trans-formed if they just spent as much time each day cleaning up their inner man, as they do washing and grooming their physical bodies. Which is more important?

The truth is we give time to the things that are really important to us. This is why Jesus said in Matthew 7:21, **"Not everyone who says to Me, 'Lord, Lord,' will enter the kingdom of heaven; but he who does the will of My Father who is in heaven."** Many call Him **"Lord,"** but how many really live under His lordship?

We tend to think of the Lord as we do other human authorities who compel us to do what they say or suffer immediate consequences. How-ever, we are in the age when the Lord is calling those who will serve Him because they love Him and they love the truth.

It says in Ecclesiastes 8:11, **"Because the sentence against an evil deed is not executed quickly, therefore the hearts of the sons of men among them are given fully to do evil."** Jesus is the Lord above all rule, authority, and dominion, but for the purpose of revealing hearts, He has chosen not to execute judgment quickly in this age. Because we are able to get away with things without swift punishment, many drift in their devotion and obedience. This reveals our true heart.

The reverse is also true. The rewards of righteousness are seldom immediate. Therefore, many drift from righteous devotion. This also reveals our true heart. Even so, the judgment day will surely come. As both Jesus and Paul explained, it will come upon the world like birth pangs upon a woman in labor. That is, as we get closer to the birth, the contractions will become more intense and more frequent.

We have been given a kingdom that cannot be shaken. We build our lives on that kingdom by obedience. It is too late to start building our houses on the rock after the storms have come, just as we are told in Psalm 32:6, **"Therefore, let everyone who is godly pray to Thee in a time when Thou mayest be found; surely in a flood of great waters they shall not reach him."** As our King Himself admonished in Luke 6:46-49:

> **"And why do you call Me, 'Lord, Lord,' and do not do what I say?**
>
> **"Everyone who comes to Me, and hears My words, and acts upon them, I will show you whom he is like:**
>
> **he is like a man building a house, who dug deep and laid a foundation upon the rock; and when a flood rose, the torrent burst against that house and could not shake it, because it had been well built.**
>
> **"But the one who has heard, and has not acted accordingly, is like a man who built a house upon the ground without any foundation; and the torrent burst against it and immediately it collapsed, and the ruin of that house was great."**

Notes:

DAY 46

Tough Love

In this age the Lord is calling us to His kingdom under His domain—we are not being forced. When He bodily returns to the earth to establish His kingdom, He will rule with a rod of iron. But in this age, He is calling those who prove their worthiness to rule with Him by their willingness to serve Him and walk in His truth, even when both the rewards for obedience, and consequences for disobedience are not immediate. This requires a walk of faith, but true faith is always obedient as we read in Romans 16:25-27:

> **Now to Him who is able to establish you according to my gospel and the preaching of Jesus Christ, according to the revelation of the mystery which has been kept secret for long ages past,**
>
> **but now is manifested, and by the Scriptures of the prophets, according to the commandment of the eternal God, has been made known to all the nations, leading to obedience of faith;**
>
> **to the only wise God, through Jesus Christ, be the glory forever. Amen.**

Of course, the greatest test of our obedience will be in regard to the difficult things He has commanded. One test is, we are to love our enemies. This is easy for those who do not have enemies, but let enemies arise and many of us will start praying for the Lord to send fire from heaven to consume them. Possibly every American who is reading this is right now thinking of the Islamic extremists who attacked the World Trade Center and the Pentagon. How can anyone love such people? God does. He loves every one of them and desires for each of them to be saved.

I believe it is important to biblically establish the difference in the mandates given to the civil government and the church. The civil government is an authority established by God, and as Paul wrote in Romans 13:4, **"for it is a minister of God to you for good. But if you do what is evil, be**

afraid; for it does not bear the sword for nothing; for it is a minister of God, an avenger who brings wrath upon the one who practices evil." The civil government is not told to love its enemies, and would actually be in disobedience by not bringing wrath upon those who do evil because it has been given the sword for that purpose. However, the church has a different mandate. We are told to love our enemies. We are in disobedience if we do not love them.

I heard a most encouraging broadcast on *Fox News*. They reported that for every attack on Muslims in the United States since September 11, there have been at least ten acts of love, kindness, and reaching out to Islamic Americans, mostly by churches. They interviewed a number of Muslims who were overwhelmed by the kindness and support they had received from their neighbors, confessing this was something they were not expecting. To me this was one of the most encouraging indicators of the health of the American church and the soul of this nation that I have heard in a long time.

It has often been reported that the man who planned the Japanese attack on Pearl Harbor, and the man who commanded the Japanese forces that day, were both educated in America. Most foreign students who come to America list two things as their most important goals when they come— to get a good education and to make American friends. Both of these Japanese, military officers received an education, but it seems they were shunned and isolated, leaving without making any real American friends. How would history have been changed if they had?

Even if history is not going to be changed by our acts of love and kindness, we are commanded to love our enemies. This in no way infers that all of the Arab and Muslim people who live in the United States, or outside of it, are enemies of America. Many are our friends, who consider such terrorist acts as an affront to their faith. Even so, we who are Christians are commanded to love even the extremists and terrorists, even those who will not receive it, but rather view it as a sign of our weakness. We are not commanded to love only those who will love us back. This is truly a difficult thing, but are we going to obey *all* that He commanded?

DAY 47

Enduring Love

Today I want to talk about the second great test of love, which is endurance. This is what the Lord referred to in His rebuke to the Church of Ephesus in Revelation 2:4-5:

'But I have this against you, that you have left your first love. 'Remember therefore from where you have fallen, and repent and do the deeds you did at first; or else I am coming to you, and will remove your lampstand out of its place—unless you repent.

The most common understanding of this term **"first love"** is they lost the passionate love for the Lord that they had in the beginning. Certainly it is rare for any married couple to maintain the fire they had for each other in the beginning of their marriage for more than a year or two. Usually marriages move from the fiery passion they have in the beginning, to a love that continually fades in passion. Most claim that this love is actually deeper and more fulfilling, but is it?

What most consider the fiery passion of love is more physical attraction than emotional, intellectual, or spiritual. Sex is a wonderful gift from God that is intended to strengthen the bond in the marriage relationship, but it is far from being the whole relationship. If the bonding does not go beyond sexual attraction to emotional, intellectual, and spiritual bonding, it will be a tenuous relationship at best.

The same is true of our relationship to the Lord. The initial fire and zeal we had when we first met Him is wonderful, but we must go on to know His heart and His ways. The more we get to know Him and His ways, the more deep confidence and faith we will have in Him. Because the fire and zeal that we have for the Lord in the beginning is not a physical attraction, there is no reason it should diminish. In fact, we should become even more excited as we get to know Him better. There is no thrill in the universe like getting to know the Lord.

153

There is a phrase some of the great saints of the last few centuries have been fond of using. It is "moving deeper into God." There have also been movements called "deeper life" movements. Those I know from these movements usually have a rich and deep relationship to the Lord that is special. However, with few exceptions (and there are some), there seems to be an unwritten rule with many of these, that the more mature you are spiritually, and the deeper your walk with the Lord, the less emotional you will be about it. I have even been told their love "goes beyond feelings," which I think is a basic deception. I do not believe any love can go beyond feelings. How would you like for your spouse to say to you, "Darling, I don't feel anything anymore, but I still love you."

I realize many immature believers exhibit their emotions or physical manifestations, as evidence of their relationship to God. Yet, even biblical references to the great angelic beings that dwell in the presence of God, and have since before the creation of the world, still tremble, marvel, and seem to constantly be in awe of the unfathomable wonders of God. After millions of years they will still be going to higher and higher levels of ecstasy and glorious wonder as they behold more and more of Him. I am sure we will all be crowding around doing the same thing.

There may be other galaxies, and worlds to behold and learn from, but there will never be anything in creation more wonderful, or inexhaustibly fulfilling, than knowing the depths of God. Stars may fade after a few million years, but the glory of God will never fade. It is not possible to truly get closer to God without getting even more excited about Him. Much of what some refer to as "the deeper life," may be learning more about God, but anyone who is truly getting closer to Him will grow in their passion for Him as well. It is impossible not to.

If we drift from the passion we first knew, it can only be because we have drifted from Him. Because the church is first and foremost His temple, when we drift from Him, we are no longer abiding in Him, and we will therefore stop manifesting Him. We can still do ministry, and learn deeper things about Him, but the true measure of our spiritual life will always be by His manifest presence in our life.

In II Corinthians 2:14 Paul talked about how he **"...manifests through us the sweet aroma of the knowledge of Him in every place."** If someone comes into the room that is growing in knowledge, it is not likely to get your attention. However, when someone enters a room, who has been in the presence of the Lord and is getting closer to Him, everyone's attention will be irresistibly drawn to them. As Paul continued in II Corinthians 3:7-11:

But if the ministry of death, in letters engraved on stones, came with glory, so that the sons of Israel could not look intently at the face of Moses because of the glory of his face, fading as it was,

how shall the ministry of the Spirit fail to be even more with glory?

For if the ministry of condemnation has glory, much more does the ministry of righteousness abound in glory.

For indeed what had glory, in this case has no glory on account of the glory that surpasses it.

For if that which fades away was with glory, much more that which remains is in glory.

Because Moses had been in the Lord's presence, he reflected so much glory that he had to put a veil over his face. We are also told here that what we should be experiencing in the New Covenant is supposed to be even better than that! One of the ultimate questions we should be asking is: where is the glory? It is in His presence. When we learn to draw close to Him and dwell in His presence, we will experience something even greater than what Moses did. Moses met with Him face-to-face, but we have Him living in us. Hebrews 12:29 tells us "...our God is a consuming fire." If we are truly getting closer to Him, the fire in our life will be growing.

Notes:

DAY 48

Enduring Faith

It seems we are now coming to the time when everyone's faith will be proven. Faith is not proven until it is tested, and the times that we are entering will test the faith of us all. This is our greatest opportunity. In the Lord every test is for the purpose of promotion, to see if we can be entrusted with more authority and power. Are you ready for the tests?

As my friend Francis Frangipane likes to say, "You never fail one of God's tests—you just keep taking it until you pass. And, every test is an open book test. You can go to the Bible and find the answer for every problem. If you have trouble finding it there, you can ask the Teacher." This is all true, and should be a great encouragement to us. We should be able to find the answer to every problem. However, finding the answer is not all there is to passing the test. We must live the answer.

For us to pass the test that comes to prove our love, we must stand in love, allowing love to control us even when we are tempted to think wrongly of others, or have the choice to do good or evil to them. Every time our love is tested it is an opportunity to grow in love. We probably all pray for the Lord to help us grow in love, but do we truly seize the opportunity to grow when the trials come as an answer to those prayers?

I know many people who have asked the Lord to give them patience, but I don't know many who asked this more than once! His answer to this prayer is to put us in circumstances that require us to grow in patience, which is very trying for those of us who don't have much patience. However, if we recognize the trials and devote ourselves to the peace and rest of the Lord, we will grow in patience.

For us to pass the test that comes to increase our faith, we must stand and walk in faith—not fear or doubt. Every test of our faith is an opportunity to grow in faith. We probably all pray for the Lord to help our faith, but do we seize the opportunity to grow in faith when the fears or doubts come? In I Corinthians 3:11-15 we are told:

> **For no man can lay a foundation other than the one which is laid, which is Jesus Christ.**
> **Now if any man builds upon the foundation with gold, silver, precious stones, wood, hay, straw,**
> **each man's work will become evident; for the day will show it, because it is to be revealed with fire; and the fire itself will test the quality of each man's work.**
> **If any man's work which he has built upon it remains, he shall receive a reward.**
> **If any man's work is burned up, he shall suffer loss; but he himself shall be saved, yet so as through fire.**

Did you ever think of the Lord as an arsonist? He lights fires in His own church just to see what we will do! His tests are not drills, but real fires. Even so, the answer to every test is basically the same—turn to Jesus. Jesus is the answer to every human problem. The answer to the love test is to behold His love for us and let it flow through us. **"We love, because He first loved us" (I John 4:19).** The answer to the faith test is to behold the Lord. If we see Him we will have faith.

While in the military and as a professional pilot, I was subjected to routine tests to determine my competency as the pilot in command. If I was well prepared, I would enter those tests with great confidence, even exuberance at being able to see my own level of skill increase under pressure. Tests in the Lord should be the same way, as James 1:2-4 states:

> **Consider it all joy, my brethren, when you encounter various trials,**
> **knowing that the testing of your faith produces endurance.**
> **And let endurance have its perfect result, that you may be perfect and complete, lacking in nothing.**

If we have joy entering trials, it is a good sign that we are ready. If we are fearful and depressed at the prospect of having our faith tested by the times we are entering, this should be a revelation to us that we are not as ready as we should be. This doesn't mean that you will not be at least a little nervous at the prospect of trials, as even the most prepared person will usually be slightly nervous entering a test. But I am talking about something more than that—I am talking about fear gripping us to the level of near panic or depression that colors our life at the prospect of what is coming. To the degree this kind of fear grips us in the face of testing can be an indication of the degree to which we are not ready for it. However, be encouraged, you still have time.

We still have time, but we cannot waste any more time. If we are not ready for what is coming, it is only because we have wasted too much time in the past, which is one thing we must determine not to do any more. We must now give ourselves to the study that we have always promised ourselves we would. We need to devote time to prayer and fellowship with the Lord and His people. We need to choose now to give our time to the true spiritual gold, silver, and precious stones instead of wasting it with what is in fact worthless. We need to pursue and develop our spiritual gifts, and the training or discipleship that we need. One of the greatest antidotes to fear is the pursuit of purpose, having a vision and step-by-step goals for their achievement. We should be occupied with that which causes our faith to grow.

The Lord is about to release the army that He has been preparing for these times. Most battles are determined by the quality of the soldiers more than anything else, and quality soldiers have confidence in the day of battle. If we are properly trained and equipped, we will be confident as we enter the times that are now upon us. If we are not confident, do not waste any more time. The fire is coming that will reveal whether our life is built on gold, silver, and precious stones, or wood, hay, and stubble. If we are ready, we will be confident. If we lack confidence, we must quickly make the necessary changes in order to get ready. The stakes are too high to waste any more time.

Notes:

DAY 49

Enduring Vision

After establishing enduring faith and enduring love, we must have an enduring vision if we are going to stay on the path to the fulfillment of our purpose. For us to have a vision that endures, it must be the vision to which God has called us. How do we know the vision is something to which God has called us?

First, it should be the deepest desire of our heart. The Lord created each one of us with a purpose before the foundation of the world. He put that purpose in our heart, and there is nothing else that will be completely fulfilling us until we are fulfilling that purpose. Living waters come from our innermost being. The deepest desire of our heart is what we have been called to.

Of course, because of sin and wickedness, or subjection to religious and control spirits that instill insecurities and/or rebellion, many have a hard time discerning what is the deepest desire of their heart. The primary way He strips away the veils that cloud our vision is by revealing His glory to us. Man was made in His image, and when we see Him and behold His glory, it calls to the deepest desire of our beings and what we were created to be.

The glory of the Lord is not just a lot of brilliant colors, but it is His character revealed through His actions. That is what we read concerning His first miracle in John 2:11, **"This beginning of His signs Jesus did in Cana of Galilee, and manifested His glory, and His disciples believed in Him."** As we behold the works of God, we can discern His ways and His nature. In them we see His mercy, His grace, His love, and sometimes His righteous judgment. We can also see His glory in nature, as the Lord stated even Solomon in all of his glory did not clothe himself as well as the Lord did the lilies of the field (see Matthew 6:28-29).

As we behold His glory in these ways, it strips away the veils that cover our true hearts and changes us so we become like Him. It is also our calling that determines the primary way we see Him. If you are called as a pastor you will see the shepherd of Jesus in everything He does. If you are called as a teacher you will see the glory of His teaching in everything He does. If you are called as an evangelist you will see in all of His teaching and works as an evangelistic call. If you are a prophet you may see the glory of prophetic revelation in them.

Of course, the one event that reveals His glory and nature more than any other is the cross. He is eternally called "the Lamb" because we will forever be seeing His glory and love in the cross. This glory of the cross is revealed in increasing layers and depth that we will not exhaust for all of eternity. Billions of years from now we will still be in awe of the cross. As we now behold the love revealed through the cross, we are compelled to become like Him, taking up our own crosses daily to give our lives to the sacrifice of service to others. As we do this He is able to trust us with more and more of His power which further reveals His glory and ways.

To become who we were created to be, we should always be looking for His glory in everything. As Elizabeth Barrett Browning once said, "Earth's crammed with heaven, and every common bush afire with God; But only he who sees, takes off his shoes—the rest sit round it and pluck blackberries." How different would our lives be if we could see?

Again, our primary goal in life should be to see His glory in everything. This is not an easy task, which is why, as a new believer I was stunned when I first read Isaiah 6:1-3:

> **In the year of King Uzziah's death, I saw the Lord sitting on a throne, lofty and exalted, with the train of His robe filling the temple.**
> **Seraphim stood above Him, each having six wings; with two he covered his face, and with two he covered his feet, and with two he flew.**
> **And one called out to another and said, "Holy, Holy, Holy, is the LORD of hosts, the whole earth is full of His glory."**

My problem with this was how the Seraphim could say that the whole earth was full of His glory. I thought of all of the wars, hatred, child abuse, racism, disease...and honestly thought this was a mistranslation. Then one day I felt the Lord speak to me and say that the reason why the Seraphim saw the whole world full of His glory was because they dwelled in His presence, and if I would dwell in His presence, I too, would see His glory in everything. I would not just see the present conditions, but I would see His plan for redeeming them and restoring the glory that He always intended to fill the earth. This put me on the path for the necessary change in my life that would be required if I was to serve in His presence.

If we are going to walk the path that reveals His glory, carrying and demonstrating the glory of His ways, His redemption, and His ultimate plan for mankind, we must start to behold His glory so that we are changed into a demonstration of it. That is your ultimate calling—to reveal the glory of the Lord.

Notes:

DAY 50

Charting Our Course Into the Future

The true Christian life is the greatest adventure and the most glorious quest that can ever be known on the earth. Nothing Hollywood has ever produced can compare with the reality of the true Christian life. There is nothing as exciting, as fulfilling, or as compelling as getting to know our King and learning His ways. When this is our daily quest, the focus and devotion of our life, we will find the path of life that is the bridge between heaven and earth. It is never too late, or too early to start this journey. As we do, we will be used to bring true life to the earth, and bring defeat to our ultimate enemy, which is death.

The goal of these "Fifty Days" devotionals is to impart a vision for what the Christian life is intended to be from an uncompromising, biblical foundation, with a historical perspective. I purposely sow into each of these devotionals some repetition and review to increase retention. My goal for writing is not literary or artistic achievement, but to promote spiritual fruitfulness and an irresistible devotion to our purpose for being on this earth.

We are living in extraordinary times. Great changes are sweeping the world. Great changes are also taking place within the church. There are some things, such as sound biblical doctrine, that must never be changed. There are other matters in the church that desperately need to be changed. In general, the structure of the modern church is more an invention of medieval institutional Christianity than the biblical model for the church. When the church rediscovers her true purpose and makes the necessary changes to fulfill it, there will be no greater force on earth, or one more relevant to the times. In fact, she will begin to live by the power of the age to come.

The changes needed to make the church relevant to the times are not just to make the church "seeker-sensitive," but to enable her to become the living, powerful force that she is called to be. The Reformation of the church has been more than a five hundred year process, but it is far from complete. In fact, there may be as much reforming left to do as has been done to date. Will this take another five hundred years? No. It can even be done in a day. As we are told in II Peter 3:8:

> **But do not let this one fact escape your notice, beloved, that with the Lord one day is as a thousand years, and a thousand years as one day.**

This implies that the Lord can do in one day what we think would take a thousand years. The Lord is certainly patient and, therefore, will probably take a little more than one day to complete this job; but the radical changes that are needed to bring the church into her full purpose can and will happen quickly.

Some of the greatest changes coming will involve the structure of church life and function. We can learn much by looking back at the first century church, however, we cannot fully understand what the church is called to be by looking at the past. We are not called to be the first century church, but the twenty-first century church.

If we are going to understand the church's full purpose, we must begin to look beyond the church to the kingdom. The Lord did not send us to preach the church, but rather the kingdom. We cannot fully understand what the church is called to be without understanding her purpose in preaching and preparing for the coming kingdom of God. As the Lord said in Matthew 24:14:

> **"And this gospel of the kingdom shall be preached in the whole world for a witness to all the nations, and then the end shall come."**

This is not the gospel of salvation, which is generally what comes to mind when we think of the gospel. Of course, we will be eternally grateful for the gospel of salvation, but the gospel that must be preached to all nations is more than this—it is the good news that Jesus is the King of kings and He is returning to rule over the earth. This is the message that must be preached to all nations before the end will come.

That His kingdom would come, and His will be done on the earth as in heaven, was the focus of the prayer He taught His people to pray, and what we have been praying for nearly two thousand years. This prayer will be answered. We are living in the times when this message will be proclaimed across the earth. Not only will this message go forth, but the foundation for His kingdom will also be laid.

To preach this message we must believe it ourselves. If we really believe it, we will begin to live in His kingdom now. To live in the kingdom we must live under the Lord's rule and authority. Is His authority growing in our lives? Are we becoming more obedient and more sensitive to His leading?

If we are abiding in His kingdom our message will not just be in words, but in demonstration of His authority and dominion. As we are told in I Corinthians 4:20, **"For the kingdom of God does not consist in words, but in power."** Unprecedented power is coming to the messengers of the kingdom to preach the message of its arrival with authority. This is what we are preparing for.

My hope for these "Fifty Days" books is that they will find their way into the hands of those answering the call to the ultimate quest, helping to encourage and keep them along the way. In the next book we will go into much more detail about the kingdom that we are called to proclaim and be citizens of. You, however, do not have to wait for the book, you can live in this reality now. We must faithfully continue to go higher, farther, and deeper, but above all things, we must become more like Him.